Where *and HOW* to Find
More Customers
When You Run Out
of Family and Friends

Written and Created by
Christie Northrup
The Lemon Aid Lady

WhereToFindCustomers.com

Design by CaseyHooperDesign.com

Published by CANet Consulting
Nauvoo, Illinois 62354

Published by CANet Consulting™

Where—and How—to Find More Customers When You Run Out of Family and Friends. Copyright 2010 by Christie Northrup. All rights reserved. No portion of this book may be reproduced, stored in a retrieval system, or transmitted in any form or by any means—electronic, mechanical, photocopy, recording, or any other—except for brief quotations in printed reviews, with our the prior written permission of the author.

Printed in the United States of America

ISBN: 1-930182-07-3

Dedicated to

Everyone who
has ever opened a lemonade stand

Table of Contents

Your Business is like a Lemonade Stand

Remember your pre-tween years, when you wanted to earn some cash but were too young to get a job? If you were like millions of other kids over the past century, you opened a lemonade stand. Why have so many kids used the lemonade stand as their first entrepreneurial endeavor?

* Kids usually look for jobs in the summer when they have time off school, and summer is synonymous with the need for cold beverages, especially those with the quenching qualities of lemonade
* A lemonade stand can be started from home; kids don't have to go anywhere!
* Start-up costs are normally funded with mom's ingredients and labor!
* Family and friends, people kids have a relationship with, are typically the customers

With such a great idea—tasty product delivered to *thirsty* people in the heat of the summer—why is the life expectancy of lemonade stands less than two hours? Because once family and friends buy a glass or two of lemonade, the kids are out of business (mom being one of the best customers, of course)!

You've grown up and your lemonade stand might be...

* Your own entrepreneurial endeavor: retail shop, professional practice, unique product, service, or invention
* Franchise: food industry, services, retail store
* Home-based business: party plan, network marketing, music teacher, child care provider, crafter or designer
* Sales representative: automobiles, real estate, insurance

Or your career may be in another of the thousands of other business ventures out there. And yet, like a lemonade stand, you must attract *thirsty* customers to buy your product or service for you to stay in business. Unlike a typical lemonade stand, however, you don't have to stand in one place and hope customers will come to you. You have hundreds of avenues that you can go out to and bring them to your stand.

For more than thirty years, I've worked with thousands of independent sales consultants; many of them would claim that the product "sold itself", but when they didn't experience the success they anticipated, they left; easy come, easy go! Additionally, I've watched numerous businesses in the towns I've lived in open shop knowing they were going to make a killing only to get discouraged because the customers didn't flock to their doors daily. As business owners, entrepreneurs and salespeople we cannot expect other people to drive business to us; it's nice when that happens, but we must be the driving force.

> You don't have to stand in one place and hope customers will come to you.

I once met a sales manager in the hospitality industry. He was frustrated that his city's tourism office wasn't doing more to bring him customers. He stated that if the tourism office did their job, he could fill the rooms at his property. This is sour thinking. I asked what he was doing to bring people to the hotel; he mentioned that he occasionally sends out e-mails. The key word here is occasionally, which is not enough activity or frequency.

While your parents might have donated the raw materials for your lemonade stand, more than likely the start-up capital for your current business endeavor came from your personal investment or savings, loans, outside investors, or from the resources of the company you represent if you're a commissioned salesperson. In all cases, an investment of time along with real effort—"sweat equity"—was a necessity. Your first customers could have been your neighbors, cousins, co-workers, and even parents (it is good to grow with whom you know, but only as long as you grow!). One thing you have in common with lemonade stands and all businesses is if you run out of customers, you'll be out of business, regardless how wonderful your "widget" or service is or how much of your time and money you've invested to start the enterprise.

Are you beginning to see how your business is like a lemonade stand? Because you...

- ❊ Are a person who wants freedom and independence to grow a business
- ❊ Know you have a great product or service
- ❊ Want to service *thirsty* people

While you're reading this book, you'll discover

- ❊ How to find *thirsty* customers by learning and living the Lemon Aid Laws for Locating Leads™
- ❊ Where to find *thirsty* customers by reading the alphabetized, reference-style lists of places *thirsty* people hang out. Keep in mind this is a generic discussion applicable to hundreds of types of businesses; not all the "wheres" will apply to you. Sprinkled throughout the alphabetized section, you'll find other "hows."

> One thing you have in common with lemonade stands and all businesses is if you run out of customers, you'll be out of business.

What does relationship-based mean?

While mass marketing has its place, consumers like to feel that they, as individuals, are important to the people they do business with. They appreciate being called by name after completing a transaction at the cash register or receiving a personal phone call alerting them about items on sale specific to their needs. As John Dewey said, quoted in Dale Carnegie's classic book *How to Win Friends and Influence People*, "The deepest urge in human nature is the desire to be important." Additionally, customers want to *know* the person from whom they purchase insurance, obtain advice on personal health, or hire to build their home.

Personal service—whether in a group or one-on-one setting—is quickly becoming a thing of the past, what with the telephone and the Internet, home shopping TV channels and mail order. Yet, like jewels, the more *rare* something is, the more *valuable* it becomes. Customer-focused relationships are valuable to you and to your customers and clients.

> As you inspire individuals to do business with you, the masses are eventually motivated to work with you.

When your business is focused on knowing a prospect's needs and then offers sweet solutions with or without your product or service, you begin to build a long-term relationship. The prospects then become your customers, who in turn refer you to others. Thus, your business multiplies and your profits increase.

Relationship-based businesses can require a significant investment of your time before you see a financial return. One of my sales leaders taught me that in the beginning, you'll do a lot of work that you won't get paid for; and when you work persistently and grow a strong, loyal customer base, you'll end up getting paid for work you've never done.

Who is the Lemon Aid Lady?

As the Lemon Aid Lady, I don't remember many of the details of my youthful lemonade stands where I sold cold beverages, probably because I didn't make any money. My first profit-producing "lemonade stand" was selling newspaper subscriptions door-to-door when I was in fifth grade. I saw an ad for subscription salespersons in a new, local paper; I called for information and was invited to the home of the publisher. When I got the directions, I knew this was quite a bike ride (obviously, I didn't have a driver's license in fifth grade). But I was determined...

I knew my parents would tell me all the reasons why selling newspaper subscriptions would not be a good idea. First, they wouldn't want me to go to a "stranger's" home, even if they drove me. And who would want to subscribe to a community paper when we already had two daily newspapers in our city? So I told them nothing about my business adventure; I just didn't want any naysayers to get in the way. I wanted to make money! And I did!

Like most lemonade stands, my business venture was short-lived; just long enough to buy Christmas presents for my five siblings, parents, and friends. But I met my goal to make money by *going out to meet customers;* not by waiting for prospects to come to me. That was the *only* way I could sell those subscriptions!

Years later, after college, marriage, and giving birth to my first son, I was looking for a way to bring some extra cash into the family coffers without having to take my son to a day care center. This was years before the average person considered being a business owner, the advent of the Internet, or ease of communication and distribution like we have today.

As I was baking cookies on St. Patrick's Day, 1980, I realized I needed more plastic containers to hold flour, sugar and leftovers: Tupperware®. So I contacted the local distributor and decided to become a Tupperware lady! For the next seventeen years I sold plastic storage containers by holding six to eight home parties a week, recruited hundreds of other sales consultants and led large sales teams as an independent sales consultant and later, as a franchised distributor with my husband. During this time, our family made several cross-country moves, and each time I had to begin my business from scratch because I knew no one in most of the cities. Yet in spite of "no friends and family" in these new areas, I grew huge customer bases and successful, nationally ranked sales teams.

> I met my goal to make money by *going out to meet customers*; not by waiting for prospects to come to me.

After I'd been a sales representative for over ten years and six moves, a guest at a home party gave me a warning as she waved her pointed index finger at me, "I'm here to tell you, when you run out of family and friends, you're going to be out of business!" I didn't want to burst her bubble by bragging that I began and continued to run my highly-successful business without knowing any family and friends from sprawling metropolitan areas to tiny hick towns! So, I just smiled politely and thanked her for her opinion. However, there was truth to her statement: without customers, businesses close!

After selling our Tupperware franchise, I founded Lemon Aid Learning Adventures to teach entrepreneurs, business owners, independent direct sales consultants, and salespersons whose relationship-based businesses depend on finding and keeping customers in unique and creative ways. I named the business in reference to that trite (but oh-so-true) saying "When life gives you lemons, make lemonade!" Only I did a paradigm shift—what I call the *TWIST*—to rephrase that saying to "When life gives you lemons, make something better from the bitter." And I've found my concept of making something better from life's bitter situations—the

> My *TWIST* on a trite saying: "When life gives you lemons, make something better from the bitter."

"lemons"—truly gives "aid" to those willing to move forward to success.

Additionally, as both a consumer and sales leader, I grew tired of the trite and tricky ways to rope people into buying something; so you won't read these techniques in this book. On the contrary, I'm going to teach you fresh, creative ideas with a Lemon Aid *TWIST*, which stands for:

The
Way
I
See
Things

Before you can change the sour situation of not having enough customers, you must shift your paradigm. That's the essence of the Lemon Aid *TWIST*. And as your perspective changes, so will your activities. You'll need to do things that will make you stand out from among the rest of the business community so prospects will notice you. This is not always comfortable but will be more profitable.

Get ready to do the Lemon Aid *TWIST* as I teach you gallons of ways to add Sweet Successes and Juicy Profits to your business!

Lemon Aid Laws for Locating Leads

Admittedly, the following laws have never been presented to any committee let alone Congress, but they are the simple steps I created and used to build large relationship-based businesses across the United States for the past thirty years. When you obediently follow them, although not in any particular order, and then create the *TWISTS* that work with your personality and product, you will attract more and more customers who love working with you because you are focused on their needs first.

When I began my selling and relationship-based business, I didn't do a lot of research on how to find leads and approach prospects. The extent of my formal training was attending sales meetings where my peers and leaders shared their experiences. But I discovered the concepts that I'm sharing with you in this book simply by going out and meeting people. Of course I met a lot of folks who didn't want to work with me. That was okay. I can honestly say I cannot remember anyone being rude. Perhaps it's because I didn't put any pressure on anyone; I only wanted to take their "temperature" to see if they were *thirsty* for my product.

> I didn't put any pressure on anyone; I only wanted to take their "temperature" to see if they were *thirsty* for my product.

When I work with my consulting clients, I find they are amazed that I know the right words to say to prospects in most situations without using scripts or salesy tricks. I explain to them that the more we do something the easier it is to do.

I have over thirty years of practice and am still learning and practicing; after all practice makes profits! Gottcha there...you thought I was going to say "perfect." But that's the problem. Sales people are so worried they don't know the perfect

> The more we do something, the easier it is to do.

words to say or the best action to take that they do nothing but complain that business is lousy. So, use the following **Lemon Aid Laws for Locating Leads,** written in layman's language and easily remembered using the accompanying initials, as you go out to find more customers.

Let's begin with Lemon Aid Law #1: **KPKP**

Know Your Products so you'll Know who your Prospects are

We took some friends to dinner at one of our favorite places as a token of appreciation for helping us do some work around our house. Even though we were very familiar with our favorite entrées, our friends were curious about other dishes and asked the server specific questions. To each inquiry the server replied, "I don't know; I haven't tried it." One of us finally suggested he dine at his own restaurant!

In other situations, we've had the opposite experience where the server gave us suggestions and described the dishes in detail, down to the seasonings! In these instances, our appetites were whetted; we were very hungry for the dishes because of the personal recommendation from the expert server.

How can you find *thirsty* people if you don't know what you have to quench their thirst? If you don't know what ingredients are in lemonade and what it tastes like, how will you be able to tell someone that it is sweet-yet-sour, and oh so refreshing to a parched throat? In marketing terms, this is known as translating the product's "features" into "benefits" to the customer. In old advertising terms, it's "selling the sizzle, not the steak."

> How can you find *thirsty* people if you don't know what you have to quench their thirst?

If you have a variety of products—as in hundreds—this can be an overwhelming task. Nonetheless, you still need to know what's in your sales arsenal. So, take one product or service at a time and learn not only its features, but also its benefits to customers; get to know one item from every product category and expand your expertise from there.

The best way to know a product is to use it! Reading about something in a catalog or on a website is nothing compared to touching and experiencing it. As you use the product for its intended purpose, do the *TWIST* so you'll also begin to think of other uses. The more familiar you are with these characteristics, the more *thirsty* prospects you'll begin to think of! For every product you have ask this question:

> If I had all the money in the world, *who* would I *buy* this item for?

If I had all the money in the world, *who* would I *buy* this item for?

This is a *TWIST* in mindset—figuratively *giving* instead of furiously *selling* because you base the decision on who you'll market to focusing on the people (individuals you personally know) or groups you want to get to know. The end result is all about the end user—who will benefit the most from your product, not solely on you who will profit from the sale.

Let's assume your product line includes hundreds of items of tools and trinkets for cooking and baking. Begin by choosing a set of mixing bowls to review. Thoroughly examine one of the bowls. You might think, "What's so great about a bowl; you can find them any place." But there are always differences, real as well as perceived:

What makes the bowl unique? Could it be the designs on the inside and outside?

Are the bowls produced in "classic" colors or are they taken from the newest seasonal palette?

Is this bowl's purpose purely functional (mixing, storing, or serving) or simply decorative (display-only purposes)?

Does the bowl have measurements on the inside or outside?

Is there a handle to hold on to while mixing?

What about non-skid "feet" on the bottom?

Is the finish designed to avoid scratches from spoons and electric beaters?

What material is the bowl made from? Is it a thick, break-resistant ceramic or lightweight plastic?

Can the bowl be used in the microwave and regular oven?

Is it dishwasher safe?

Does it come with a lid?

Can you freeze food in it?

Do recipes come with the bowl?

Was the bowl made to last for generations or is it trendy, even disposable?

I use the example of the bowl because it's a simple, common object. You might have been surprised to learn of the various characteristics of bowls! You'll be just as surprised to examine the products and services in your line; all have both features and benefits that are waiting for the right customer.

And as you **Know** your **Product,** you'll really get to **Know** who your *thirsty* **Prospects** are, and as you become an expert on your products, you'll be an expert in your industry so prospects and customers will look to as a resource for all items related to your products—in and out of your line.

Now that you know who your *thirsty* prospects are, let's start with who you already know:

Lemon Aid Law #2: **GNO**

Grow with who/what you Know

While the object of this book is to teach you *how* to find customers *when* you run out of family and friends, you certainly do not want to forget the people you already know: your family and friends!

Many sales "trainers" teach you the concept of creating a F.R.A.N.K. list which stands for:

Friends
Relatives
Associates
Neighbors
Kids' acquaintances

> Promote your business to those with whom you already have a relationship, then grow from there either through referrals or by moving on.

This is a good exercise *as long as you determine if they are thirsty* for what you offer, instead of begging and bribing them to do business with you because of your association. You definitely want to promote your business to those with whom you already have a relationship, then grow from there either through referrals or by moving on.

Our family has made many moves over the years, which gave me the opportunity to meet more customers across the continent. With each move, I'd meet my new neighbors and introduce them to my business. After all, most people want to know "what you do." When we bought our first home, I was too pre-occupied with moving in and setting up house to meet my neighbors right away. Sure enough, within a couple of weeks, my neighbor across the street came by to invite me to a home party with the company I was a consultant for! I was thoroughly embarrassed and mad...at myself, not at the neighbor. She had been so *thirsty* for my company's product, she found a consultant through the phone book when I was right across the street!

After working with business owners and sales professionals for over thirty years, I've discovered that most are on two opposite ends of the spectrum. Either they overwhelm their warm market and grill them to death with sales pitches or, they're so afraid their family will feel obligated to buy insurance, cars, housewares, scrapbooks, or whatever product or service these reps offer that they don't tell their relatives *anything*. Surely, there is a way to grow with a "warm market" of people you know. So, let's do the *TWIST* and **forget Frank**!

Rather, work with W.I.L.M.A.

Consider the people you already know and ask yourself:

Who
Is a
Likely
Marketing
Audience?

Obviously, you don't always know *who* could be *thirsty*, so you need to combine the *who you know* with the *what you know*.

For example, you've just opened a car repair service. As you're developing your marketing plan and prospect list, you remember your neighbor's celebration of making the last payment on his five-year-old SUV, and his desire to *not* buy another car for a while. He is now a *thirsty* prospect for maintenance services and repairs that often accompany an aged car!

> You can create a *thirst* for your product or service if you do the *TWIST*.

Conversely, if your cousin just bought a brand-new sedan he might not be *thirsty* for repair service, unless he gets involved in an accident and needs body work done. So while he might not be in your WILMA group, keep him updated about your business interest by being interested in what he does. For example, offer him a maintenance special for oil changes. See...you can create a *thirst* for your product or service if you do the *TWIST*.

And remember, if a prospect is not receptive to your offers, respect her decision; don't *TWIST* any arms! Attempting to "overcome the objection" only strengthens the prospect's resolve to NOT buy your product or service. So, leave them happy and move on to another prospect!

Now that you've identified *thirsty* groups of prospects, it's time to learn:

Lemon Aid Law #3: **HO HO**

Hang Out
where your leads
Hang Out

If I provided you the funds to grow an orchard full of lemon trees, and depended on you to find the best location, trusting your decision would yield a great return on my investment, which of the following areas would you choose to develop the orchard?

Albany, New York

Anchorage, Alaska

Anaheim, California

The answer should be obvious because lemon trees require a warm climate with no frost; Albany and Anchorage do not qualify! Of course, you could grow lemon trees indoors, but trying to do so would take much more money and time since you'd have to invest in a climate-controlled building; you're better off working where the climate is best. This is the essence of hanging out where your leads hang out!

> Work where the customer climate is best.

Notice I didn't say to *wait* for leads to come to you. In any relationship business, the world is your "store." Even if you're based in a "brick and mortar" business, you can implement many of the activities you'll read about in this book to *go out* and find *thirsty* customers. And what better place is there to go than where the leads are!

In order to discover where *your* leads hang out, you need to refer to the previous Lemon Aid Laws, KPKP and GNO. Once you've decided this, consider where you

> *Go out* and find *thirsty* customers. Where will you hang out?

can "hang out." Let's say you own a hair salon and are looking for *thirsty* customers; where would you go? You might say "everywhere" because most people have hair that needs cutting and styling. Ahhh...but that's not exactly true. Some people don't have hair! And there are others who never cut theirs!

So, think back to the WILMA principle (GNO Law)...who is most likely to need your services? Go for the obvious first. High school girls going to proms and dances would be a very *thirsty* audience for you. Can you advertise in the school bulletin? In such cases you don't actually have to BE someplace to "hang out" as long as your presence is felt.

Another obvious *thirsty* market for hair stylists would be brides desiring to look stunning on their wedding day. Hang out by being an exhibitor at a bridal show—where brides-to-be hang out. You would certainly choose this over exhibiting at a custom car show, not that people at that show wouldn't be *thirsty,* but because you're looking for WILMAS: the most *likely* marketing audience.

> Who is most likely to need your services? Go for the obvious first.

Now, let's consider the not-so-obvious. I recently moved to a new city and one of the biggest fears I had was leaving my wonderful stylist, Peggy, back in Texas. And wouldn't you know it, my hair grows so fast and because I have short hair, I can't wait very long in between cuts. A lot of people moving to new areas have the same fear; this group of people could be a *thirsty* audience for your business.

So, where do people new to the community "hang out?" If your town has an organization for new members, you can attend those meetings. Check with your Chamber of Commerce or real estate association to see if they are aware of gatherings for new people. In fact, I met my new stylist in Illinois at a Chamber of Commerce meeting.

Now do the *TWIST:* What else can you do to hang out with these prospects? Consider hanging a sign on your building or marquee: "New to town? Let me take care of your crown!" Okay, that's a bit silly, but it caught your attention, didn't it? This book is full of other "wheres"— places to hang out where your leads hang out.

Remember to review and use all the Lemon Aid Laws for Locating Leads so you'll know how to identify *thirsty* people, begin conversations and relationships.

As you do the HO HO, you need to do more than simply hang out, you've got to look, listen, and learn which is:

Lemon Aid Law #4: **LLL**

Look, Listen, Learn

Whenever I take my grandkids on outings and we approach a street or parking lot, I always have them stop and look for vehicles that could run us over, and listen for something approaching that we're not yet able to see. Maybe you remember being taught the stop, look, and listen principle to protect you before crossing a street.

This Lemon Aid Law is a *TWIST* on that rule because you don't want to stop finding customers, you want to go out and then:

Look at what people are doing. You'll be surprised at what their actions are "screaming," which could indicate a *thirst* for your product.

Listen not only to *what* people say, but to *how* they are saying it.

Learn information about the individuals that could connect them to your product or service.

Being alert to these actions will bring you gallons of business. One venue I often use is where consumers abound: the grocery store. I always **look** at what people put in their grocery baskets, and even though they don't *say* anything to me, I can **listen** to them by what their purchases and actions *convey*. By taking these two actions, I can **learn** what their needs might be. If their needs are connected to my product or service, I open my mouth and visit with them.

To illustrate this, let's imagine the waiting area of your local quick oil change shop where you, a professional home and office organizer, are waiting for your car to be serviced. While you're thumbing through the raggedy, old magazines on the table,

the thought comes to you to approach the owner of the shop, who obviously could use your expertise, and might perhaps do a trade for your service.

Instead, you take the time to **look, listen** and **learn** about other customers.

> Never stop looking for customers.

You notice a professional-looking couple on the sofa next to you and can't help but overhear their conversation, in which they're lamenting that they keep forgetting to have their oil changed because they haven't had the time to organize their files or their electronic calendars. Bingo! They could potentially be *thirsty* customers. Now's the time to mentally determine if what you offer could benefit this couple, which is accomplished with:

Lemon Aid Law #5: **MM**

Develop a
Matchmaker Mentality

Do you remember playing the card "match game" when you were in early grade school? There are many versions, but the one I remember included cards with pictures of objects as well as cards with letters of the alphabet. Both sets of cards had the same design on the back and were mixed up and placed face down on a table. The object was to turn over a picture of, say, a banana and then the find the card with the letter "B" so you'd have a match. In the beginning, finding matches was a challenge until more turns were taken and more cards were turned up. Then you'd remember where the matches were. The game came to an end as matches became easier to find due to the process of elimination.

Finding customers is like playing the match game; you have a product or service and you're matching what you have to *thirsty* prospects. The difference between the game and this concept is you must continually keep a Matchmaker Mentality, because you'll always be finding new cards (customers and prospects) to match your products. In fact, you might find some matches you'd have never thought of in places you never imagined.

> You must continually keep a Matchmaker Mentality.

If you're a piano teacher, you know what your product is: teaching music lessons. Let's say you decide to attend a home schooling conference, an audience you've identified as *thirsty*. You're hanging out at the conference and attending breakout sessions, and as you visit with other conference attendees—mostly parents—you look for those who want their children to take piano lessons. Not drum, bugle, violin, or trumpet lessons. You might talk to a lot of people and "turn over" some of these conversations until you have the matches you're looking for.

Or, perhaps you own an insurance agency and decide to Hang Out where your leads Hang Out by displaying at a home and garden show. You're looking specifically for home owners, not renters. So, as visitors come to your table and you give out advertising souvenirs, you want to spend time visiting only with people who own homes. As in the case of the piano teacher, you're going to have to turn over a number of conversations to find a match for your service.

Keep playing the match game! Ask any young kid who has played the game with cards and they'll report that they have to turn over several sets of cards before discovering a match. Yet, the fun is in the finding and doing, which is why you need to keep a continual **Matchmaker Mentality**.

> You're going to have to turn over a number of conversations to find a match for your service.

You'll discover matches for your product by opening up conversations with prospects which brings us to:

Lemon Aid Law #6: **CCCCCC**

Convert Casual Conversations into Committed Customers with a Compliment

This law is a big HOW: How to open up conversations with strangers; it's quite easy to "C" by opening conversations with compliments. I'm not talking only about commenting on someone's outward appearance, although those are nice words and good observations. The best compliments go beyond the dress; begin with Lemon Aid Law #5 (LLL: Look, Listen, Learn) and then open a conversation using a compliment with a *TWIST:* in Lemon Aid language this means to give people a S.Q.U.E.E.Z.E:

Statement
Questions
Usually
Elicit
Explanations and
Zap
Excuses

Don't tell any English professors, but I made up a new component of the English language: *Statement Questions.* These are comments—asked in question form—that generate an immediate response which explains more about the prospect. These simple statements usually begin with:

"Looks like..."
"You seem to..."
"You must..."
"I bet..."
"Sounds like..."

Here are some examples, the italicized adjectives and nouns can be changed to some of the suggestions in parentheses:

* Looks like you're a *great English teacher* (patient dad, fun mom, organized executive, busy student, kind friend)
* You seem to know how to *decorate* (lead, shop, coordinate colors, care for others)
* You must love *great literature* (fine dining, chick flicks, photography, writing, reading, researching)
* I bet *health* is important to you (education, family, work, exercise, cleanliness)
* Sounds like you *enjoy your job* (love your kids, appreciate art, understand finance)

As you open your conversations with these Statement Questions—the SQUEEZE—you get a feel for the "ripeness" of a prospect as she responds in agreement: "Yes, I love teaching teenagers."

Or with a definite rebuttal: "I only teach because I worked so hard to get my English degree."

Either way, you'll quickly learn more about the prospect from this simple SQUEEZE, and with her response, some of the excuses to not do business with you are zapped in advance. I'm not talking about the sales trainer who teaches you how to "overcome objections," which ends up being a sales gimmick. Instead, you already know this person does or doesn't love her job, so you're a step ahead.

> Use the SQUEEZE to get a feel for the "ripeness" of a prospect.

For example, let's say you have a business opportunity to offer this teacher, and she assures you that the only reason she's teaching is because of the investment she's made in her education. When you mention an alternative or addition to her current career, she's already admitted she's not passionate about her position, so the possible excuse she could give you of "I love my job" is not valid. Now, the approach is not to use this as evidence against her by saying, "You said you didn't like teaching" but instead a way to find out if she's *thirsty* for your opportunity.

My target audience for years has been women—that's a broad audience (definitely no pun intended!). If I noticed a woman with a cartful of kids and groceries in the check-out line ahead of me, I'd comment: "Looks like you're a busy mom!"

I might get a response of: "These aren't all mine! I'm watching my neighbor's kids while she's in the hospital with a new baby."

Then I can give another compliment, "Wow...you're a nice neighbor!"

The conversation can continue as I find out more information about her. Perhaps she says, "I'm actually paying my neighbor back! She watched my kids while my husband and I went away for our anniversary a month ago."

I'm now discovering little bits of information that might lead to a business conversation as I reply: "How many years have you been married?"

"Ten!"

"Congratulations! Most of my customers are like you: married more than five years."

Now she'll probably ask you a question about your last comment. DO NOT GIVE A 30 SECOND COMMERCIAL! I know...this is what sales trainers have taught for years! It's a good thing I'm an educator, not a trainer. The difference is I teach you to think, not to be robotic and give everyone the same answer! So, when she asks a question, give short answers so she will...

* Listen (after all, she did the asking)
* Want to know more with future questions

Let's return to a possible dialogue:

"What kind of business are you in?"

"Protecting families."

"Against what?"

"Financial hardships."

Can you see how the conversation has shifted to what you do and has connected the two of you together? Throughout the conversation, think of two more Cs: **Commonalities Connect**. In this scenario, her family situation has a commonality with most of your customers: married more than five years. You've just connected her with your financial services product; something she could be *thirsty* for.

> Your heart has to be in the conversation!

Now, these comments are obviously suggestions; I'm not one to teach scripts because you never know what the other person is going to say. Don't you love it when telemarketers call and your response throws them off because it's not part of the company script? My favorite is when I'm asked "How are you?" and I reply, "Horrible! I've been very ill." The script tells the rep to say, "That's nice" and move on. (Or if the sales representative is really listening, he realizes that's not what he should have said and he then becomes flustered.)

That's the beauty of the CCCCCC Law. Your heart has to be in the conversation! You have to be focused on the person, and while the conversations are intended to teach you how to find *thirsty* customers, chances are you'll engage in a nice conversation without bringing up any business because you don't perceive the person as a WILMA.

However, if you do, you need to be sure to gather contact information for future follow through. Let's return to the grocery store line (yes...if she has kids the conversation is not going to go smoothly and quietly!) as the possible prospect asks: "Financial hardships?"

> Be sure to gather contact information for future follow through.

"Yes, like unemployment, disability, illness, even the death of a spouse."

With this statement you're telling her in a conversational way what you do, and she might respond:

"My brother-in-law has been out of work for six months. Can you help him?"
By now the kids are rowdy (even though this conversation could be less than a minute long), and her turn at the check out is approaching.

So you ask her, "Do you have a business card?"

She might pull out a card showing she's a nurse at the hospital or counselor at a school (both of which will give you more reasons to talk to her for referrals). Or, she might not have a card at all, so you simply ask for a phone number and e-mail address so you contact her. This is how I politely and casually ask for information: "*If you'd like to give me your name and phone number or e-mail address, I can contact you to get your brother-in-law's information.*"

Or, if she were to be the *thirsty* prospect I'd ask, "Looks like it's your turn to have your groceries checked, *if you'd like to give me your name, phone, and e-mail address I'm happy to call you to tomorrow.*"

I then add, "I'll also give you my card so you know how to get in touch with me if you want to call me first."

In place of a business card, I prefer to give post cards, handouts, or a fun advertisement souvenir (see explanations of each in the alphabetical reference section of this book). This shows you're a credible person and if the prospect absolutely refuses to give any information but could be *thirsty* she is able to contact you and sometimes will. Honestly, the only time I was rejected from getting personal information was when I was going through security at an airport and the Transportation Security Administration employee at the airport was intrigued by the magnets I wear in my shoes. When I explained the health and comfort benefits, he was curious; however, he was not allowed to receive gifts or give out personal information. Too bad, because the screeners so often ask about things I carry in my suitcase and brief case!

> Politely and casually ask for name and phone number or email.

I also act "low key" in these conversations. My view is that I have something great to offer, so I don't need to be anxious or pushy. I keep calm and in turn people respond. Or, if they don't, it's no loss to me.

You only stand to gain by opening up conversations with prospective customers. If they don't respond to your compliment, reject your offer, or walk away, so what? You'll probably never see them again anyway.

That's why it's important, no crucial, that you always use:

Lemon Aid Law #7: **BB**

Be Bold

As I was writing this section, I wanted the title to really stand out, so I **boldfaced** the "Bs". The title now stands out so you'll know what's discussed in this section with a quick glance.

In your marketing efforts, you must **be bold** so you stand out from the crowd. And believe me, the market is crowded. You can **be bold** with your product, demonstration, dress, name, icon, decorations, websites, advertisements, promotions, offers, and more. These will certainly cause you to stand out if they are bold enough from the rest.

> **Be bold** so you stand out from the crowd.

One way to demonstrate your **boldness,** especially in a relationship-based business, is to boldly go where others do not go by opening your mouth and following through.

This includes talking to someone you meet at a book club who clearly needs what you offer; gathering the contact information of a *thirsty* prospect you met at your son's soccer game; complimenting a professional you met at a networking group; or any other situation where you're meeting potential prospects using the other Lemon Aid Laws for Locating Leads. And after the conversation or contact, you actually call, visit or e-mail to continue the process, assess, then bless, the person with your product or service.

Being bold means you open your mouth, ears, and heart...and are willing to be rejected because you know the sweet solution you offer is greater than the feeling of fear or intimidation you might experience. You see, practicing the other Lemon Aid Laws is simple in comparison with this one. You can examine your product; look, listen, and learn who or what could be a perfect match; hang out where

thirsty leads might hang out; and then, if you stop there, even with other elements, all your efforts could be worthless if you don't follow up and continue the relationship you've begun to build.

> Boldly go where others do not go by opening your mouth and following through.

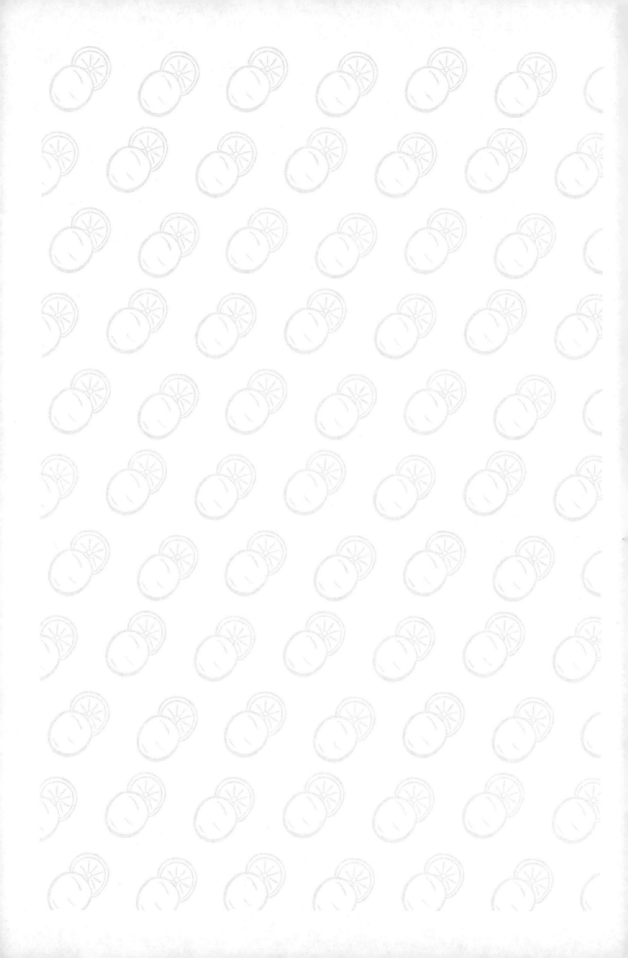

Lemon Aid Lead Alphabet

All lemon trees began with a seed although not all seeds which were planted took root and became trees. Likewise, all customers in your company were a lead at one time even though not all leads became customers. You'll always need to find bushels of leads if you want to build a consistent customer base.

While you can count all the seeds in a lemon, you'll never be able to count all the lemons that come from one seed. After all, one seed can grow into a tree with countless lemons which also contain seeds that can become lemon trees. And you'll never be able to count all the relationships you'll gain from just one *thirsty* lead.

Something else I cannot count is all the times I've heard salespeople and business owners say, "Well, I didn't make any sales, but I planted a lot of seeds." Planting seeds, and finding leads, is only the first step in gaining customers. The following alphabetical, reference-style section of the book teaches you how and where to find *thirsty* prospects—leads—for your business. Use the gallons of ideas along with the Lemon Aid Laws for Locating Leads to nurture, water, weed, fertilize, and even prune your customers so you'll grow a sweet, successful business full of juicy profits.

> While you can count all the seeds in a lemon, you'll never be able to count all the lemons that come from one seed—or all the customers that will grow from one lead!

✳ Advertising

Everything you read in this book comes down to advertising—telling the world what you do and encouraging them to purchase your product or service. However, the focus here is not on marketing to the masses with a massive advertising budget, rather you'll learn ways to influence and inspire individuals at little or no cost. Once you have groups of loyal, committed customers, they will lead you to people they know and your business will continue to grow.

Traditionally, the most effective kind of advertising has been word-of-mouth. People tend to believe their friends with whom they have things in common and have mutual trust.

Women are especially great at word-of-mouth advertising. They love to tell others about their great finds, particularly when they discover a wonderful value. This is the idea behind the successful direct selling marketing model. Instead of investing in expensive advertising, companies pay independent consultants to open their mouths and tell their friends and family about a product. However, these representatives—like all business owners and sales professionals—must also learn about finding customers because their prospects quickly dry up after they've run out of family and friends.

Additionally, in our age of technology many people never share verbal conversation. Rather they text, e-mail or post written, audio, or video messages to their Facebook, Twitter, or YouTube accounts. When people meet you in these mediums

and like what they hear and see, they pass your information on to their friends with a few clicks. This is called "buzz" or "viral" marketing and you can find customers this way, again with virtually no cost to you.

Inexpensive, paid advertising targeted to your *thirsty* prospects can work well in some cases; however, the return ratio may not justify the expense. One key rule of advertising, free or paid, is to have ads repeated several times. For example, if you advertise on the radio, you'll want to schedule several spots, often in a short amount of time, so your prospects will hear it over and over. If you choose written media like daily and weekly newspapers or monthly magazines, repeating the message multiple times will eventually draw a multitude of customers who will watch for your ads in each publication.

> Ads must be simple to read, understand, and respond to.

If you do want to pay for advertising, you should consult an advertising professional. Your prospects are smart; they are able to tell if you know what you're doing by the kinds of ads you produce. Some companies have TV ads that appear to be amateurish for a homey feel. Even these kinds of ads take a lot of work to create!

If you choose to create your own ads, make them simple to read, understand, and respond to. Use catchy headlines that call for immediate action. In the section on flyers I teach an incredibly inexpensive way to do advertising that can be very effective.

Now let's do a *TWIST* on advertising:

Take advantage of others' advertising. Be aware of potential customers who need your product because of what *they* sell. For example, If you sell Items used for kitchen organization, contact people who are advertising catering services, cooking schools, or restaurants. You'll find ads for these businesses in the newspapers, direct mail pieces, telephone books, and on line banner or pay-for-click advertising. Another potential customer base for your organizing products or services would be someone who sells makeup or crafts. They might need something to carry their smaller products in. Could your product fill their need? If so, you might be able to do some cross promoting with them.

☀Advertising Souvenirs

My parents have a unique ice cream scoop with a wood handle and stainless steel edge for scooping. Engraved on the scoop is a message from the local funeral home. Every time I use this tool when working in my mom's kitchen, I laugh about why a funeral home needs to advertise. Yet, I'm sure when the time comes that those services are needed, we'll already have scooped up our choice...

The business of advertising specialties (my TWIST is to call them souvenirs) is a huge industry because we all enjoy gifts from vendors and suppliers which, in the advertising world, are referred to as "trash and trinkets."

> **Your souvenir should be related to your product.**

When you choose a giveaway like this, relate it to your service. Let's say you own a carpet cleaning business. Give your prospects something to clean with like a small brush to dust their computer screens and keyboards.

Calendars are gifts that prospects can use all year long. However, customize each month with reminder text pertaining to your business. If you're a dentist, place a sticker on the dates where your patients should have their teeth cleaned.

Pens are probably the most common ad souvenir because they are such a common tool. Further, you can give customers your pens and they might use it to autograph their credit card receipt at the department store and unintentionally leave it there. The next customer could pick up the pen with your ad on it and decide she needs your service. Pens are a traveling advertisement, so be sure that in addition to your contact information, you include your tag line and actually advertise your business.

Advertising souvenirs are Fun-der-ful gifts that can build on a marketing campaign. For example, if you're opening up a new insurance business, send targeted prospects a can opener with the words, "We're open for business so you can be fully covered."

✳ Affiliate Program

Affiliate programs are basically referral programs. The difference is that most affiliate programs are connected with your website and everything is automated so that once a customer or professional affiliate registers, your shopping cart vendor keeps track of all the purchases made through each affiliate's unique URL.

The automation of an affiliate program is not difficult if you have the right shopping cart. However, affiliate programs work best when education, communication, inspiration, and even contests and incentives are provided. This can be as simple as a monthly e-mail listing the top-paid affiliates. I like to give my affiliates previews of what's coming up before new products and promotions are announced to the general public.

I love to offer my affiliate programs to my loyal customers so each time they shop on my site, they earn a commission on their personal purchases. Some sites don't allow this. However, my thought is affiliates are the first to make purchases, so why not reward them when they buy and when their referrals buy?

Many sites have a minimum payout, usually calculated monthly. I can only guess what the rationale is behind this; it seems to encourage sales by threatening an affiliate. But I disagree with this tactic: I want all my affiliates to taste their success every month. If they have to wait a few months to accumulate a minimum bonus, they might be reluctant to promote the program.

> I want all my affiliates to taste their success every month.

Pay Pal is an absolute must. In the beginning I thought of sending checks with a personal note. I soon learned the best motivator is getting an e-mail essentially saying, "You have money waiting for you in your PayPal account."

As always, you can do a *TWIST* on affiliate programs. Not only can you provide the programs for your customers, you can also become an affiliate for other websites and products you love as you earn referral rewards for yourself. These can really add up!

❋ Airplanes

On an airplane, you could have a captive audience; however, don't make any-one feel like they are a prisoner to your marketing message. Instead get to know your "seat neighbor" if he is open to conversation. (Hint: If he gives quick answers to your questions and keeps focused on his book or computer, let him fly in peace!)

Use the Laws for Locating Leads as you visit, always staying focused on the other person. If your product or service is a possible match, be prepared with literature and business cards and ask for their contact information. If you carry samples of your products to give away or even sell, this is a good opportunity.

As an author, I carry copies of my books in my computer bag. One time I neglected to replenish my supply. On a flight from Dallas to Phoenix, I met a business owner who was very curious about my book. Because I did not have a copy with me, she followed me to the baggage claim area where my luggage had books packed inside. She gladly paid me for a resource that can now be a real benefit to her business.

Perhaps your seat neighbor works in your city and flies home on the weekends. She might give you referrals for people she knows in your town as well as her own city.

Place some of your literature in the seat pockets where the magazines are kept. Or, put the literature inside the on-board publications. Leave a note informing the readers that you can do business with them no matter where they live.

❋ Apartment Complexes

Check with owners or managers of apartment complexes to see if you can get some exposure with the tenants, particularly for items specific to apartment dwell-ers such as renters insurance. Many complexes have clubhouses where flyers can be posted. Also, ask if they have tenant newsletters that you can advertise in. Or volunteer to write a column in the newsletter as the expert in your field. Complexes that are locally owned might trade advertising for your product.

Many apartment managers put together tenant fairs in the clubhouse where vendors can set up tables on a specific date. The vendors might be charged a nominal fee, which is revenue for the complex. Most importantly, this is a great resource so the tenants can be serviced on site. If this option is not available, ask if you can set up a product display in an area of the clubhouse one day a month, preferably on a pay day weekend when tenants are coming to the clubhouse to pay their rent.

> Set up product displays on pay days.

Get to know the managers and, if allowed by their employer, give them samples of your product for their personal use. Ask if they will provide you with an ongoing list of people moving in and out.

For new move-ins you can donate a gift or gift certificate, especially if the complex provides welcome baskets to new tenants. The people moving out might be moving to their first home, and may be *thirsty* for your product if it is needed by home owners.

✳ Attention Getters

This is any way of getting people to *approach you* about your product or service. In this situation, people are already curious. If you're carrying samples or products to sell, you have a target audience. When you reply to their request, be careful not to give a lengthy advertisement (no "30-second commercials"). Rather, give them a few details at a time. Because they were the ones who asked, they'll also be eager to listen to your response if you spoon feed them rather than dump gallons of information. They asked for your information; be careful not to overwhelm them and subsequently turn them off.

Listen carefully (LLL); someone might be curious about your product by giving YOU a compliment instead of inquiring about your product. For example, when someone is taking an application and needs personal information such as your year of birth. When she looks at you and exclaims, "You look much younger than that!" the door is now open for you to share your skin care, hair service, or health product/procedure with her. This is the very reason you must be a billboard for you products at all times as you'll never know who you're going to influence!

✳ Attraction Alphabet

How many times a week are you asked for your name, address, account number, reservation locator, and such where you need to spell out the information for clarity? You've probably given the usual explanation, "B as in boy," "T as in Tom," "F as in Frank," and so on.

> Attract customers when you're the customer.

When you create an Attraction Alphabet for your business, you can attract prospects in these situations where you are normally the customer. Look at your product and industry and identify each letter of the alphabet with one of these.

The other day, Melissa, one of my TelAdventure students, won a gift during class. She represents an exclusive skin care line. As she was spelling her name to me over the phone, she gave the typical, "M as in Mary, S as in Sam," and so on. After she finished, I suggested she do a switch with any or all of the following statements along with choosing a question/commentary in parentheses:

> **M** as in makeup (What kind do you use?)
> **E** as in erase (I can teach you how to erase your wrinkles.)
> **L** as in lipstick (Are you looking for some new colors?)
> **I** as in investment (Do you ever invest in yourself?)
> **S** as in skin (What does your skin say about you?)
> **S** as in soft (You won't believe how soft your skin will feel!)
> **A** as in appearance (Are you ready to enhance yours?)

Please don't use more than one or two in a conversation or else the shared information can be really jumbled! This is such a simple, unique, and entertaining way to find new customers!

✳ Auctions

These have become a common way for groups to raise funds either as a traditional or silent auction. Often these types of auctions are linked to a fund raising dinner, craft show, expo or other event.

Donating to these causes can be beneficial as long as you go beyond just giving something away. If the auction is a traditional live event and you are able to attend, watch the people who are bidding on your product or service. Do you know any of them? Did you meet them during the pre-auction mingle time? Do you have their business cards so you can let them know your products are available for purchase if their bid is not chosen?

After the winning bidder is chosen, introduce yourself and exchange contact information for future service. They'll be happy to have a connection with the source of the prize and will now be able to contact you for future purchases or assistance. If you're not invited or able to attend the auction, be sure the organizer gives you the contact information of the winning bidder.

> Donate products for auctions with the agreement you'll get the contact information of the winner and bidders.

Silent auctions are when donated items are displayed along with a sheet of paper for bidders to write their name, bid, and phone number (a *must*, so that they can be contacted if they have the winning bid). Before giving your donation, have an agreement with the organizer that you'll donate the gift as long as you get the list of all bidders. Now you can contact those whose bids were not chosen to let them know they can still get your product. You might want to offer a special "bid price." For example, if the retail cost of your gift is $50 and a person made a $25 bid, offer a purchase price of $35 which is higher than her low bid but not as much as the retail price.

✳ Auto Repair Shops

This venue is not only for men. Many women maintain their own cars. If your *thirsty* audience includes either gender, you could find customers here.

✳ Badges

Badges with catchy sayings will cause people to be *curious* about your business and *ask you* what the badge means. A question on the badge is even more effective than just a statement because people will *come to you* with an answer or comment. You're going about everyday activities—shopping at the store, volunteering at school, taking a walk with your family, etc.—so you might as well give your business some fun, easy, and profitable exposure at the same time. You just never know who has been looking for you and your product!

Wear a badge with your company name on it. If your company provides you with a name tag or badge, wear it—it's a great attention getter! When you're walking down the aisles of a store, aren't you attracted to people with name tags? Those people stand out from the rest, don't they?

Now, as you approach this person with the name tag, you probably think she works at the store. But as you get closer, you notice the name tag doesn't represent the store...she's not an employee. So, you look even closer, don't you? This is human nature. Now you know her name and company. Could she be a *thirsty* prospect for you? Are you *thirsty* for her company's product?

Likewise, you'll want to stand apart from the crowd, so always wear your name tag when you're out and about and dressed to do business. However, don't wear your company badge if you're in your grubbies and sweats because first impressions are lasting; you'll give the wrong impression of your normally-professional image.

Combining your company badge with a creative badge also works well. Some of my most fun business experiences happened when I've stopped at the store on my way home, not even thinking about my business, and someone would ask me about my business because of the badges I wore! Badges are no-brainers!

❋ Bake Sales

Bake sales attract hungry people, perhaps those who are hungry for your product! You can host your own bake sale, or more simply, donate baked goods to an organization's sale and promote your product/service at the same time.

Before you sigh because you don't have the time or exper-tise to bake, do the *TWIST:* You can donate baked goods that are NOT baked by you. Every grocery store has a bakery department, if it's no more than the boxed cookie aisle!

> You can donate baked goods that are not baked by you.

Purchase or bake your donation (you can give more than one), and then choose one of these ways to promote your business:

1. Attach your business card along with a *purchase or free item offer* (this way, the purchaser needs to contact you!).

2. Attach the recipe for the baked goods along with your business card and free item or purchase offer (people love and keep recipes so be sure your contact information is on this).

3. If your business is marketing products such as bags, bowls, baskets, plates, mugs, or other products that the baked goods can be placed in, donate the product and attach the recipe, business card, and a catalog or mini catalog. The group sets the price for your product, which could be lower than the retail value. This is an attractive presentation that will attract more buyers and attention!

4. Offer your business as a bake sale venue. If a local club is raising funds with a bake sale, hold it at your office or retail location. It's particularly good if you get regular traffic. Be sure the organization lists not only your address but also business name on all their advertisements.

5. Offer matching funds. Propose to donate a percentage of the funds raised up to a certain limit. The group will surely remember you, your company, and your generosity.

If your business offers fundraisers, visit any bake sales you see advertised. Introduce yourself to the organizers and set an appointment to explain what you offer for their next fund raising event. While you're there, be sure to purchase some baked goods or make a donation. This will leave a lasting impression.

✳ Banks

Banks are where you take money (in or out), but they can also be a place where you can make money as you find new customers.

Business owners really need to know the staff at their local banks. In some cases you'll be securing loans and bankers like to know the people they lend to. For the discussions in this book; however, you want to find more *thirsty* customers! Many employees at the bank could become your customers or lead you to other *thirsty* people.

> Do the employees at your bank know you well enough to refer other customers to you?

I live in a small town, which is a plus for building relationships. The folks at our local bank know us very well, and have at times called us with referrals from other bank customers because they know us and what our business is all about. Do the employees at your bank know you well enough to refer other customers to you?

Additionally, some banks invite their customers to participate in business expos so they can become acquainted with other bank customers who own businesses—you never know who might need each others' products or services.

Ask your bank if they offer these types of events. If not, suggest they try it. After all, this shows yet another no-cost benefit that banks can give and banks want their business customers to be successful and profitable.

✳ Barter

When I walked into the hair salon last week, my stylist was excited to see I had a copy of the new cookbook I had just written in my purse. She immediately said, "Don't pay me for your hair cut today; I just want your cookbooks to give as gifts!"

At my last appointment, I gave her a copy of my *CookINspiration* cookbook as a token of appreciation. She enjoyed the book and then gave it to a friend who was getting married. I was thrilled to barter with her not only because I saved forty bucks of cash, the difference between the cost of the books and her service, but also because she'll give my books as gifts and more people will become *thirsty* customers.

Bartering is trading your product/service for the product/service of another. As I just illustrated, this not only saves on cash flow, but also adds more customers to your base. When you are in need of a product/service, go to a person in that business and suggest bartering. This way both of you have a new customer and you can also cross-promote each other's business through referrals. This works well for any two people who are willing to trade. Just be sure you both keep good records and receipts and check with your tax advisor; bartering can be subject to income tax.

> Bartering saves cash in your pocket and adds customers to your business.

You can barter for services and products you use in your business (advertising, printing, office supplies, etc.) as well as items needed in your personal life. For years, I did not pay cash for any hair services or manicures for me or my family. Everything was bartered! At one point, my hairdresser was remodeling her home. She traded with other customers for everything from counter tops to windows to carpets! Bartering broadens your business base!

One caution, though: Only barter for what you need. I've seen people fill up their homes and offices with so much stuff in the name of the great deal they bartered for, but things which they didn't really want or need.

The bottom line is, you're still paying for the products because you have the cost of your own goods. Even when you barter a service for a product, calculate how

much you could earn in place of bartering. Attaching a true dollar figure is a good way to decide if you should trade your valuable time or product for something you might not need.

In addition to trading with people you already know, you can find many on line sites to barter with people across the world. Remember to trade retail price for retail price. This way you both end up getting the other's service at your wholesale cost; you'll never pay retail again!

✻ Beauty Salons/Barber Shops

You just read how I bartered with my hair stylist. When you're having your hair cut or other services in the salon, you can have great interaction with your stylist as well as the neighboring stylists and clients. Depending on how long the service takes, you can give a casual sales presentation simply though chit-chatty conversation!

> You can give a casual sales presentation simply though chit-chatty conversation!

Refer to the *Laws for Locating Leads* while you listen to the dialogs going on around you. The salon is one place women really spill their guts!

When your stylist understands how you service customers, she can also refer other clients to you as she visits with them. For example, if you own an interior design firm and one of your stylist's clients mentions she's ready for a redo and remodel of her home, your stylist can provide an immediate commercial for you, especially if she's experienced your service.

If you're a chiropractor and your stylist complains a lot about her "aching back," offer to barter your service so she has a better back and you'll have great hair. And the next time her neighboring stylist talks about having a bad back, she can send you a referral.

You can also leave a souvenir at your stylist's station. Anything from a pen to a product catalog, as long as it's something useful (otherwise, it will be annoying). When her clients are in the chair and see the souvenir or sample, the conversation will turn to *you* and your business.

✳ Bills

Put a flyer, business card, or other marketing piece in the envelope when paying your bills. These companies gave you sales information when they sent the bill to you, so why not return the favor. You never know who will be opening the envelope. Keep the weight of the envelope to one stamp so the bill is not returned to you for insufficient postage and is not credited to your account on time.

✳ Bingo

In many parts of the country, people flock to bingo halls and spend a lot of money playing the game. So, why not have a free bingo at your place of business (or rent a meeting room)? Be sure to advertise this heavily. You can request on line registration so you have an idea of how many guests to expect and to limit the number if this is too popular.

In between the rounds of bingo, you can give quick presentations about your product and offer special discounts. Of course, you will award the winners with your product (great use of excess or outdated—yet new and useable—inventory) or service rather than cash.

> In between the rounds of bingo, give quick presentations about your product and offer special discounts.

You can purchase bingo supplies at party outlet stores. To make this more fun, combine the efforts with companies you do cross promotions with or invite consultants in your company or agents in your office to join forces with you.

✳ Birthdays

Have you ever been dining in a casual restaurant and suddenly bells ring, pans clang, or whistles blow while all the servers gather around a table singing a fun version of *Happy Birthday*? That's a signal that someone at that table is celebrating a birthday (whether they like it or not!).

One evening we were dining when the singing began. The restaurant was not very crowded and the birthday celebration was at the table next to us, so my husband and I joined in the singing. Everyone was excited that we'd invite ourselves to the party. After the noise level diminished, we began a conversation with the family and although we were nearly a thousand miles from home, we discovered that the man's brother lived in our hometown and had done some auto body repair work for us. You never know who you'll meet!

> Give birthday wishes and see if they're a *thirsty* prospect.

Be prepared with Happy Birthday cards—including a gift certificate for your products—to give to the "birthday person." Or, if you have a fun *advertising souvenir* or a sample of your products with a festive ribbon tied around it, you can deliver an extra gift and greeting to a fellow diner.

Be observant of other opportunities where you see birthdays being celebrated. Adults who are marking a milestone (30-40-50-60 years and so on) might wear a T-shirt, badge, or tiara promoting the fact. Wish them a Happy Birthday and see if they're a *thirsty* prospect.

If you're with groups of people whom you don't know—such as a tour group—announce you're looking for a birthday person to give a gift to. You'll be surprised at how easy it is to find people celebrating their special day!

✻ Bookmarks

Bookmarks are essentially business cards in a different size and shape. They can have a higher perceived value because they have a use beyond providing mere contact information on a card, which often end up in the circular file! Anytime you would give a business card, hand your prospect a bookmark instead. They'll hold on to it and use it!

✻ Bulletin Boards

While you can post flyers and business cards on bulletin boards (read about both concepts in those sections of this book), find more customers by reading what is already posted on bulletin boards.

Could these individuals be *thirsty* customers for your product or service? What about cross-promotion possibilities? Do you need the products and services of these individuals and see an opportunity for bartering? Could your product benefit them while they're selling their product? If you have a business opportunity, these people might want to hear what you have to offer in addition to—or instead of—what they are currently involved in.

Get in the habit of looking for bulletin boards at stores, libraries, community centers, restaurants, print shops, and all other establishments you visit.

✳ Bumper Stickers

Putting a bumper sticker on your car should bump up both contacts and sales. As a customer, one of my pet peeves is seeing a bumper sticker for a company I'd like to do business with, but without any contact information!

So, stick to these suggestions:

1. Add your contact information, preferably just a phone number. Nearly everyone uses cell phones and if a prospect is walking through a parking lot and sees a logo of a company she's *thirsty* for shown on your bumper sticker, she can dial your number immediately. If you're available, you could set up an instant appointment to meet close by. Yes...you might have some security concerns about this; after all we live in a scary society at times. However, what's the difference between putting your phone number on a bumper sticker or on thousands of catalogs or in a newspaper ad? If you want exposure, you need to be bold yet careful.

> Bumper stickers can bump up sales and get customers sticking to you.

2. List at least a website if you don't show a phone number (but remember that web addresses can be difficult to remember or write down while driving).

3. When your bumper sticker looks awful, take it off of your car. Sloppy advertising communicates sloppy products and service.

4. Give bumper stickers to your customers to place on their cars, campers, motorcycles or bathroom mirror—wherever they want!

5. Consider magnetic bumper stickers.

✳ Business Associates

If you're starting your business while you're employed at another job, and there is not conflict of interest between the two, let those with whom you currently work know about your new enterprise.

In many cases, co-workers are like a second family. You know them sometimes better than you want to, and a lot of times, you also have knowledge of their families and associates and what they could be *thirsty* for. Do not hesitate to share your wares!

If part of your business is to find other sales representatives, this is a great pool of prospects.

Additionally, those people with whom you, a spouse, or associate have worked with in the past should also be contacted. Relationship-based businesses should begin with the relationships you've already built.

✳ Business Cards

When you think of business cards, you probably think of creating and giving your own cards to prospects and customers, and I'll share some tips about this. For my *TWIST*, I'll also give ideas on gathering cards from others.

Give business cards freely: This provides a professional image in an inexpensive way. Make a goal to give out a certain number of your business cards each day; leave a trail of them everywhere you go!

Whenever you are asked to give someone your name, address, etc. when doing a business transaction (dry cleaners, doctors, etc.), give them a business card rather than dictating your information. Many stores request zip codes so they can track where their customers live. Give them your card; it can create some curiosity!

Include a business card with all your transactions. When you hand a cashier your payment, give her a business card. When you leave a restaurant, leave your card along with a tip. Whenever you meet someone, give them a card!

Enclose a business card with ALL your correspondence, even when mailing bills. Real people open mail; you never know who has been waiting for you to appear! If you're sending personal letters, send your business card along to remind your friends and family about your business.

Be sure your card looks professional with your company's logo, your name, phone, e-mail, and website. Addresses are optional and if your business is based at home, it's best to omit that for security purposes.

Magnetize your business card if you want people to keep it. The best way is to purchase sheets of magnets. These are usually less expensive at a craft store rather than an office supply store. Use rubber cement or permanent spray adhesive, mount the card on the magnet sheet, cut it out, and you have a business card they'll keep. Many advertising specialty companies offer printing direct to magnets which are quite affordable.

> Your business card can create curiosity and attract *thirsty* customers.

Business cards as bookmarks: I read a lot, and found that business cards make great bookmarks. When I put them in books I've checked out of the library—and just "forget" to remove the card when I return the book—my card becomes another way of meeting people. The next person who checks out the book has a free bookmark along with my contact and business information! As previously mentioned, write a note that encourages them to call you, such as "Redeem this card for 10% off your first purchase."

The last word about giving business cards is my favorite thing to do. Not only because it attracts more customers but because I'm giving something sincere which puts smiles on faces: a compliment!

TWIST **your business card into a "Compliment Card"** by writing a personalized compliment on the back (or in some "white space" of the card if you've printed on both sides).

The compliment could be: "Thanks for keeping my water glass filled" for restaurant servers. Or, "I appreciate the extra pillows on the bed..." for hotel housekeepers.

> Compliments are so very valuable that people will keep the card.

Compliments are so very valuable that people will keep the card. Will they call you? Maybe, maybe not. Perhaps when they're showing their co-workers, family, or friends that they received a written compliment one of those people will be curious about the printing on the card, not just the hand written note.

And if the recipient of the compliment card never calls you, she will surely recall the compliment and you every time she reads it! Talk about adding value!

Free lunch drawings: Many restaurants offer them (I love free lunches!). Diners are invited to put business cards into a bowl and once a week (or month) a free lunch winner is drawn.

To increase your chances of winning a free lunch and more customers, use these tips:

1. Add a note to the card with a free offer if they call you or visit your website (you'll need a special page in this case; one that will collect their information and electronically dispense the freebie). Write the note with a different color of pen so the writing will stand out.

2. Use attention-getting stickers on your cards because they are felt as well as seen.

3. Attach a piece of wrapped candy or gum to your card. Remember, real people are choosing the winning cards. Even if yours is not chosen as the winner, the person handling the cards will be drawn to the candy. While she's unwrapping the treat, she's reading your card, and if she's a WILMA, you could soon be servicing a new customer.

4. If one of your advertising souvenirs is small and contains your contact information, (which it should) place that in the bowl!

5. Instead of printing your cards on the regular business card size, super size it to a 4" x 6". You can add photos and a bigger ad about your business. Fold this one in half when you put it in the bowl.

Gathering Business Cards: This is THE proactive means of obtaining prospects' contact information! You'll really draw more customers to you if you do this *TWIST* and gather—not just give—business cards. If I had my choice, I'd gather business cards rather than give them because when I have a prospect's contact information, I am in control of the contacting. If I only give my card, I don't know if the recipient will keep it, let alone contact me. Always ask for a business card in return for yours if the atmosphere is conducive to that request (a grocery clerk probably doesn't have a business card handy to exchange but an administrative assistant would).

> You'll really draw more customers to you if you do this *TWIST* and gather – not just give – business cards.

More than a free lunch. Here's one of my favorite ways to gather *gallons* of cards: After dropping your card in the bowl for a free lunch and other promotions, ask the manager or owner of the establishment what is done with the cards after a winner is chosen. Some places use the cards to contact potential customers, as they should. Yet, you'll be surprised to discover that most places throw them away! If this is the case, ask him if you can take the cards home with you. You can also offer to donate a bonus gift—a gift certificate for your product—to the winner of the free lunches in exchange for the cards.

Once you have the cards, carefully review the information and sort to discover who will be the *thirsty* candidates for what you offer. When you contact these folks, you can explain that you got their card from the restaurant's bowl, or simply state, "Your business card was passed on to me from one of my friends."

If a restaurant doesn't already sponsor a drawing, volunteer to do so. Agree to buy a gift certificate for the price of lunch. You can begin by doing a monthly drawing to keep your costs down, but do gather the cards at least once a week. This is an inexpensive way to collect a lot of names, but you need to review the cards and contact the prospects as I've earlier indicated.

Instead of calling the prospects, you might want to send an e-mail to introduce yourself.

You can contact businesses other than restaurants depending on your product. For example, if you sell health food items, talk to a health club. If you sell products

related to knowledge and learning, talk to a library about your business and what you can do for the institution. If your *thirsty* audience is parents, go where parents hang out—pre-schools, doctor's offices, sports fields, etc.

✳ BYOBB: Be your own Billboard

A major part of building relationships is getting people to know you! The way you dress, talk, drive, write, all these things are posted for the world to see! When you become a "product of your product" your prospects do not need to be told to be sold; they can see it because they've had a sample—intentional or otherwise—of your personal billboard.

If your product is health related and you never exercise, eat properly, or take the supplement you're trying to promote, the message you're posting to the world is "I just want your money!"

Conversely, if your company is a graphic design firm and all your company literature, stationery, website and other communication tools are top notch, you have a great billboard.

If your product is something you can wear such as make up, skin care, jewelry, or clothing, be sure it's on your personal billboard! Hair stylists have a great opportunity to brag on themselves by keeping their hair trimmed, colored, and styled nicely. I know stylists don't usually cut their own hair, but when the over-all appearance is sharp grooming, you have the perfect billboard.

Logo wear—either on your clothes, shoes, sunglasses, brief case or other visible item—is another tool to non-verbally promote your business on your billboard!

✳ Campgrounds

When you do finally get away from it all, take some of it with you. That means always using your product to be a living advertisement. If you enjoy the outdoors, going camping is a great release. This is also opportunity for informal business contacts, ones that can open many doors.

If you camp at a campground, you know you're not really getting away from it all. You have neighbors that are actually closer than the ones next door at home. But, because the atmosphere is so relaxed, people don't seem to mind. In fact, because the stress level is so low, meeting others and visiting is really enjoyable. Inevitably, the conversation will turn to where you are from and what you do for a living. If you have a product/service that you are using while on this get-away trip, all the better. If not, get the name and phone number of your new friend(s) and be sure to contact them when you get back to the real world. A relaxed atmosphere can really be a blessing and advertisement for your business.

✳ Cars

Your car can be your mobile billboard, which is great because your business will get exposure in front of people you might not otherwise meet when you go on trips, visit vendors outside of your area, or even attend special events to which people from all over flock. On the other hand, when your car is in your own driveway, people you don't know—including your neighbors—will learn what your business is all about.

Promotional items that are better than bumper stickers include **vinyl car clings** for windows and **magnetic billboards** for car doors. The latter is great because they are easily moved from vehicle to vehicle.

Windshield shades keep the scorching heat out of your car and can also attract people to your business. Some of my clients tell me they place several copies of their sales literature and business cards under the windshield wiper blades with a sign "Please take a brochure/card/catalog."

> Your car can be your mobile billboard.

License plate holders with logos and contact details have also added more customers to many businesses. One incident related to me was a prospect who left her phone number on the windshield of a car whose license plate trim advertised a company she wanted to do business with, asking for the sales representative to call her. See why it's important to have the contact information available to prospects?

Bumper stickers with your company's logo and marketing tag: Here's a personal experience about a bumper sticker. My husband and I were stopped at a red light. The car in front of us had a bumper sticker that read "If you want to make money every time you pick up the phone, call me." Well, the offer sounded unique, and I wanted more information. But, guess what? The bumper sticker contained no phone number! How was I going to call him? My husband sped up and exclaimed that if we gently rear ended his car, we would then get his name and phone number!

Whichever car methods you choose, be sure people can clearly see your phone number or website and company name. This way, even when you're driving down the freeway, a potential customer will know how to get in touch with you. But a word of caution: Be sure you display your very best driving manners whenever you use these ideas.

One day I was driving through a small town, the speed limit being 25 miles-per-hour through the whole village. The driver of a truck from a lawn service company tailgated me the entire distance of the city and made numerous gestures for me to move over, but I was simply obeying the law. Now, do you think I'd ever call that company to take care of my lawn? Wouldn't it have been funny if it had been MY house that he was driving to? He wouldn't have had a job in that town after all.

If you use your car as an "ad-mobile," always keep it clean. I bring this point up because my car is my office on wheels and it can get rather messy. Prospects can judge a business by a car, so take my advice, and so will I!

❈ Car Washes

As you drive down the street in your ad-mobile, watch for organizations sponsoring car washes as fund raising projects. They're easy to spot when the teenagers are standing in the street waving large poster boards in your sight! Pull over and support the fundraiser.

But that's not the end! You can use car washes to find customers:

1. If your business offers a percentage of profits to groups when they sell your product as a fund raiser, talk to the organizer of the group and find out how much money they've made so far. Sometimes the amount is minimal. Discuss how your fund raising service (you might need to set an appointment at a later date if the leader is busy managing the crew) can generate funds for the group. Even if the organizer does not schedule something with you immediately, she might need your product or service in her personal life. Remember to recommend that.

2. Does your place of business have a parking lot where you can sponsor the car wash fund raiser? Invite your customers to drive by and get a wash. They'll perceive you as civic minded while the organizing group's promotions will drive referrals from their promoting efforts right to your parking lot where you can offer complimentary or low-cost refreshments along with your business information.

3. Now combine the two ideas above: Attract new customers by hiring the teenage car washers to stand out in the street with posters offering a free car wash in your parking lot. As the drivers bring their cars in, ask them to fill out a form for gift certificate drawings for your business, free estimate on a service, or other related gift. You can give each driver a goody bag with candies (great for the kiddies in the car) and a sample of your product or an advertising souvenir.

✳ Christmas Card List

You think you've talked to everyone, and that all your leads have been exhausted. Wait...let me recommend a rather warm prospect list that you usually use only during the cold time of the year. You send Christmas cards, don't you? Okay... maybe you only e-mail celebratory greetings of any sort. That list will work, too. In fact, since I've had a presence on Facebook, I've connected with hundreds of people I haven't heard from in years, now my celebration list, which includes Christmas, has grown immensely.

As you read this, it's probably not during the hectic holiday season, so why not create your own holiday: send a letter (you have plenty examples from reading what others have sent you in the past), and after giving a personal and family update, report about your business. Enclose a business card (this is a great time for the magnetic type) and any literature you have that would make sense (without costing dollars) to mail.

You never know which one of these acquaintances has been *thirsty* for what you offer or might know a *thirsty* person!

✳ Clubs

People join clubs for friendship, information, and to provide service. Most clubs meet on a regular basis, usually monthly, and the person in charge of planning the meetings sometimes has a difficult time coming up with interesting agendas to drive attendance.

Here's where you come in: You volunteer to be the guest speaker at their next meeting. Here's how:

1. First, you need to find the clubs who are *thirsty* for what you offer, which is not necessarily your product or service, but particularly your information and expertise. Where do you find them? Check your local newspaper; most have a weekly section which lists clubs and their meeting times, places, topics and contact person. Sometimes this section is under the "Community Calendar."

2. Read each club's notes carefully. The group's name might not tell you the entire story. What topics do they address? What could you offer to enhance a topic that is related to your expertise and connected with your business?

3. Call the contact person. Identify yourself as a business owner or representative of your company and that you are available to bring a no-fee presentation to her group titled _____. (Okay, now you've got to come up with a simple, yet catchy title that will explain your presentation and how it relates to the club's purpose.)

4. Your presentation is to educate the club members about your topic—it is not to give a sales pitch. However, if you are doing a demonstration, by all means, use your products; you'll create a *thirst* for them.

   Now, let's take a closer look: If you own a cleaning company which markets natural home maintenance products and have volunteered to present a class called *Maid at Home,* you would certainly use your company's tools to show window cleaning and floor polishing tips. Believe me, the audience will be impressed without feeling pressured. This is the approach you should use even during the sales process. The difference is, instead of asking for the sale, you'll be giving away products.

5. Do a drawing using pre-printed forms, which gives a professional look, but could be perceived as "salesy" if you don't position it correctly. You could also hand out blank 3"x 5" cards and ask everyone to write their name on it. Invite them to add an e-mail address if they'd like to receive other powerful cleaning ideas in their e-mail box once a month (this is how you'll begin to grow a subscriber base for an electronic newsletter). You can also ask them to jot down what they liked best about your presentation and what questions they still have about the topic. This shows what they are *thirsty* for.

6. The drawing gift will be your product/service. Additionally, have printed literature and a fun advertising souvenir for everyone. They'll certainly remember you after this!

7. People will come up after and tell you how appreciative they are for the information. Some may even ask how they can purchase your products. Pull their card out and jot this information down so you can

follow through. If they have a specific request, write that down on their card; let them see you write it so they know they will receive preferential treatment from you.

8. Of course, the follow through is critical on this. Just like any other lead-generating idea, you can get snowed under with leads, or you may have received none. Regardless, make a goal to do this frequently, about once a month. Soon, you might have organizations contacting you!

✳ Consulting

Offer a free consultation about your service/product. This is a low-key way to make an impressive one-on-one presentation. Many people say "no" to something they really want/need because they think that just having you explain the system to them will cost money.

Call your presentation a "no-fee consultation". This is less threatening than saying "Let's set up an appointment so I can tell you all about my product." Show the benefit to the customer! The term consulting is very *value added*.

When I was a sales manager for a plastic housewares company, I offered, at no charge for my expertise, a service called "Custom Kitchen Planning." I went into kitchens and mapped out exactly which products would fit in the individual's cupboards for specific items. The products saved a lot of space because of their design and saved money by keeping the food fresh longer. Some people shied away from this free service because they knew they would have to pay for the products, which was a sizeable investment. They also thought that, in addition, they would be paying me a large hourly fee. But, when I let them know I had "no-fee consulting," they were very eager to have me come over. These customers became some of my very best referrals because they saw that I really cared about them.

> "Complimentary" or "no-fee" are value-enhanced words.

Using the word "free" when referring to your time, puts little or no value on you and your time, but the terms "complimentary" or "no-fee" are value-enhanced. And, your time is actually your most valuable commodity. People will appreciate your consulting more.

As your calendar becomes filled with no-fee consulting sessions, you'll want to begin to charge for your expertise, or include it when a purchase is made.

✳ Contests

Entice new customers by offering contests connected to your purpose. One of the best examples I've seen using this idea is my good friend and client, Joyce Mathie, owner of Sergent Steam™ in Salt Lake City, Utah. Joyce's product is an incredibly amazing steam cleaning machine that I learned I cannot live without! I met Joyce through my mother, who had never met Joyce in person but saw her regularly on a morning TV program and suggested I buy the machine. Joyce and I met and discovered we needed each other's services.

> Contests must correlate with your product as well as gather contact information from everyone who enters.

Each month, Joyce paid for a promotional spot and also announced a contest. One month she was looking for the absolutely filthiest shower in the state; another was the contest to discover the dirtiest car.

People entered the contest by submitting pictures, and the winner received a complimentary steam cleaning, live on TV! Of course, those who did not win the free service became prospects that Joyce and her sales team would contact for personal sales demonstrations.

Joyce's sales representatives also do in-home party-type presentations: Each guest is asked to bring a specific dirty item, mimicking the contest she promotes across the state.

You can do similar contests. Now, you always want the contest to correlate with your product as well as gather contact information from everyone who enters. For example, if you own a sporting goods store and want to attract more golf customers, fill a large tub or tank with golf balls and invite customers to guess how many balls are in the container. The entry form needs to have a place to list their name, phone and e-mail address so you can contact the winners and prospects. After all, every entrant can be winner.

✳ Conversations

As you read the hundreds of "wheres" and "hows" in this book, you might mentally think you're not able to use some of them because of where you live, the type of product you represent, your personality, your budget; the list of exceptions goes on. True, you will find some concepts that are more useable and useful than others for your personality, product, and prospects. However, listening to, participating in, and opening up conversations is the one concept that everyone who wants to build relationships can and must use and perfect. After all, if you cannot engage in meaningful conversations, your chances of developing a successful, thriving, relationship-based business are greatly reduced. Yes, this is true even if much of your business is promoted and transacted on the Internet. In reality, composing and responding to e-mails should be conversational in its own cyberspace way.

> Everyone who wants to build relationships must perfect the art of conversations.

In the section on the *Lemon Aid Laws for Locating Leads*, I taught you how to "Convert Casual Conversations into Committed Customers with a Compliment and Commonalities." You can review that segment along with the other Lemon Aid Laws because what lead generation, prospect attention and customer retention boil down to is looking, listening, and learning (ah...another Lemon Aid Law!) to the sour situations these groups of people and more importantly, individuals, are experiencing. You are then in a position to craft a customized message to determine if they are *thirsty* to learn about your product or service by inviting them to experience what you're offering. This process begins as you are bold without being overbearing and thus engaging in personal conversation!

✳ Copy Shops

As you implement the ideas in this book, you'll be making a few trips to the local copy shop for photocopying.

Have you ever noticed that the machines have a sign warning you to "Take Your Original"? This is so you don't forget and then have to remake the copy of your flyer, advertisement, gift certificates, door prize slips, and whatever else you might have photocopied.

Time to do the *TWIST*: Leave your original in the machine! (Or at least a copy of what you copied.)

Leave the piece FACE UP so the paper can be read at a glance. You never know who is going to use that machine next! And you just left them an advertisement about your business...

> Remember to leave a copy of your advertisement in the machine.

Suppose your product is skincare. A bride-to-be (who of course wants to look her best on the big day) uses the machine after you to make copies of her guest list, and she reads your flyer, takes the paper and gives you a call.

I've found that the locally-owned shops love to have a display of their customers' flyers. So, whatever you copy to promote your business, hang up a copy for the public to see, and check out the other flyers that are there!

✴ Corporate Gift Giving

Many companies spend a lot of money on gifts for their employees and/or customers. Specialty companies and boutiques have catalogs full of gifts for appreciation and incentives, so why not create your own "Corporate Gift Giving Campaign" with local businesses? People like to deal with people they know, so start with companies that you do business with.

Most companies do not want to pay the retail prices, so if you are a sales rep for a company, check with the management to see if a corporate plan is already in place; if not, suggest one. In any case, you might have to give up some of your profit, but the sales volume will more than make up for it.

Baskets and sets of products are very popular for gift giving. You can customize your product to fit a specific business need. Gift certificates are another popular alternative.

I know of a sales consultant who was number one nationwide in her company because she showed the local bank how to use her product as an incentive for people opening new accounts. Do a lot of *TWISTs* on this idea; you'll see very lucrative results!

This is also a good possibility for bartering in full or in part.

✳ Coupons

Coupons indicate a money-saving opportunity! They are especially effective to encourage first-time buyers. I like to *do money off the purchase* of a certain dollar amount, for instance $5.00 off the purchase of $25.00 regularly-priced merchandise.

Coupons are a wonderful idea if you're going door-to-door, participating in shows and events, or just to give out as a "complimentary gift" when you meet someone.

If you have a seminar planned, have coupons for free tickets available to hand out. Stipulate that they must call ahead to get the tickets so you'll know how many guests to expect.

Use some of the great software programs available for a professional look, and print an expiration date. The closer the date, the sooner they'll take action. Print coupons on a brightly-colored, heavier paper stock. The size should be a bit irregular so that the coupon doesn't get mixed in with everything else that is "standard" sized.

Coupon distribution: You could use this in conjunction with many of the ideas in this book. Depending on the cost of your catalog or literature, you might attach one of these pieces to the coupon and include your website address as well. After all, when your customers see what you offer, they'll be more inclined to redeem the coupon. Make the buying process as easy as possible, with no extra strings attached. On line coupon redemption is a plus if you have those capabilities.

But what if someone calls you and the expiration date on the coupon has passed? Tell them you have a current coupon you can give them, rather than extending what they have. This way, you are creating urgency to place the order now! Always keep current coupons circulating.

✳ Cross-promotion

I recently made a plane reservation with American Airlines. After the agent gave me my confirmation number and our transaction was complete, she said that she could now transfer me to Hertz so I could rent a car at my destination. My husband was meeting me at the airport, so I didn't need that service. But, if I had needed a rental car, I could have made that reservation in the same phone call. This is an example of cross-promoting products, when two companies complement—but not compete with—each other in a common cause.

How can you cross promote? Think of a product, company, or another business that will be enhanced by your product. For example, if you represent a grocery shopping service, your customers probably will be overstocked with groceries. They might need more storage containers, or they might need a new pantry built. Contact companies who sell or represent these products. Is your business children's books? Cross promote with someone who owns a preschool or day care.

Make arrangements to give coupons or other offers to your associate's customers. Sharing customer bases could also be beneficial, depending on your business arrangements. I never allow other companies to use my database of customers, but if I'm a fan of a product, I'll promote on my websites or other marketing channels. Companies you are an affiliate for and those who are affiliates in a program you've created are prime candidates for cross-promoting.

✳ Data Base

A company's customer and prospect data base is the real value of its business. That's why you want to build relationships with a lot of people, so you'll always have groups of *thirsty* prospects to market to.

Whenever you sell anything to anyone, gather the purchaser's contact information. First, so you can write a thank you note (that's impressive). Next, so you can keep in touch to be she loves what she purchased, Third, so you can continue to update customers and prospects on new products and promotions.

> **Whenever you sell anything to anyone, gather the purchaser's contact information.**

So, customer databases are important. But what about marketing to the data base of other companies, including your competitors without buying their list? I've done this before and it works well. I met a presenter at a marketing symposium who was just starting her business and was looking for a *thirsty* audience. Although we are technically competitors because we're both paid presenters, I liked her audio program and thought my clients would appreciate my new friend's information.

Here's what we did. I composed a letter from me introducing my friend along with a special webpage on my site where my customers could read about my friend's program. My office mailed the letters and billed my new friend for the postage and labor. My friend never saw or touched my customers' information. If my customers

made a purchase my friend gave me a referral fee for the purchase. Everyone benefited here: my customers who were *thirsty* for more business tips got them, my friend expanded her business, and I earned some referral credit.

✳ Day Care Centers

If your product/service caters to children and their parents, you have a great target audience at day care centers. This is particularly wonderful if what you offer is something that both the center and the parents need. This way, you can barter with the owner in exchange for advertising and exposure while either meeting the parents in person or through written or on line communication.

Let's say that your product is a family organization system that can be a tool both for the family as well as the school. If the owner is really *thirsty*, give her a system to display and use. She'll be a terrific advocate for what she loves. The parents will then become *thirsty* to have one in their own homes, and the owner can give you their contact information for your follow through.

If you are a consultant for a direct sales company with a kid-friendly product, this is a place to be. You can give the owner a designated dollar amount of products for allowing you to have a display of products and mini demonstrations at specified times. Begin to establish a relationship with the owner and the parents by scheduling one week—two or three times a year—where you are on site as the parents bring their children or take them home. Maintain a consistent presence. Decide on a time period, usually no more than two weeks, when all the sales generated and new demonstrations scheduled from the parents would give the owner credit toward product for the school. Award her as if she had a demonstration. Encourage her to get additional orders from people away from the day care center as well. This idea is not just for toys. It will work for any child/parent-related item.

Remember that parents are usually in a rush and won't have a lot of time to visit with you. You can incorporate a drawing so that you get their name and phone number. Also, encourage parents to take the catalogs to their work, family, and neighborhoods to gather orders for the center. Award the parent getting the most orders/largest amount of sales some of your products. An important key is to let parents know credit from the sales will go toward providing items for the center

which will benefit *their* children. Everyone can be a winner here: the parents, the children, the owner, and you!

Now, a *TWIST* on a full display is to feature only one of your key products. In situations where the customers don't have a lot of time to spend looking at a display, promote one item to the parents and then give free merchandise to the owner according to the amount of sales.

> Volunteer to write a column in the newsletter where you'll share pertinent ideas and information with the parents.

If the center has a newsletter, put regular notices in about you and your products. Rather than insert just an advertisement, volunteer to write a column in the newsletter where you'll share pertinent ideas and information with the parents. Now you're an expert in their eyes.

Hang a poster or flyer advertising your product. You can give the owner your product in exchange for allowing you to promote your business in these ways. The more the owners have your product for use for the children, the more the children want, the more the parents buy.

As always, the goal here is to get new leads. I've had some day care displays where the sales were not so great, but I was able to service the parents, who in turn scheduled demonstrations with me, which resulted in more sales, customers, and profits.

✳ Delivery People

As a business owner or sales representative, you probably have packages delivered to your home or office quite frequently. Do your UPS, postal carrier, and FedEx delivery persons know what your business is? These dedicated people might be very *thirsty* for your product or service, or they could know people who are since they're in a lot of homes and businesses in your town (even if only to greet people at the door as they drop off packages). They probably have a lot of non-confidential information that could be of value to you, such as who is moving to the vacant office building and may need your construction crew for remodeling. Or, who was in a car accident last week and is looking for a new vehicle and maybe a different insurance company? Do what my thoughtful husband does and offer them a

bottle of water on a hot day or go out to their truck if they have multiple packages for you and give them a hand. Get to know these folks; you'll find they could deliver more than boxes and envelopes.

Delivery people might service other people in the same line of business as you are—your competitors. If I were a betting person, I'd wager that none of those business people have talked to these couriers about their product, which is why you should. Consider this. When your business is thriving, you use delivery services more frequently for incoming and outgoing packages, creating more commerce for their companies. I've provided products to several of our delivery persons over the years simply by telling them what we do and then asking if they need my business like I need theirs.

> Get to know these folks; they could deliver customers to your business.

There are other people delivering merchandise to your home: furniture, appliances, flowers, and pizza! Do a *TWIST* and give the delivery persons your sales literature and/or samples of your product. Get their home or cell phone numbers and names so you can contact them during their personal time. They might not be the *thirsty* folks, but because they are literally in the doors of hundreds of others, they might know who is *thirsty*.

✳ Demonstrations

The old adage, "It sells itself" is just not true. Whatever you offer prospects has greater impact when demonstrated in some way such as test driving a car rather than looking at pictures in a brochure; flipping through pages of a book instead of reading the promotional text of a mailer, chewing food samples rather than examining ingredients on a label. Products don't just march into homes, offices, and other destinations where your product will be used or your service will be rendered.

In most cases, quick, informal demonstrations will be the avenue where you'll find customers who line up to do business with you. The best demonstrations are those that allow a prospect to *experience* your product or service so you don't have to use a lot of words to *explain.* This is where you combine sensory with the story, with or without words such as the *scent* of perfume, the *design* of furniture, the *savor* of food or the *feel* of an automobile.

> As you visually and verbally demonstrate, allow the prospect to participate.

As you visually and verbally demonstrate, allow the prospect to participate. When she slices the tomato in paper thin slices with your razor-sharp knife or he cleans the leather interior of his car with your unique cleaner, your words pale in comparison. Allow the prospect to be a participative demonstrator and soon he'll be the owner of your product.

✳ Directories

When you signed up for the weekly bowling league, you might have received a directory of all the players in the league so if you need a substitute, you'd have a list of people to call. Or, maybe your home owners association publishes an annual directory of all the residents. These directories can be electronic or hard copy and are very useful when you need to connect with people you have a connection to. Would these be *thirsty* prospects for your business?

Certainly you'll want to use discretion and professionalism with this information so you're not looked upon as a scary solicitor. I suggest using the directories in tandem with personal contact you've already had. "June, remember me from the block party? I own Awesome Awnings, and you mentioned you needed an awning for your patio." Or, use the directory to mail information on your business. People are not as threatened by a piece of paper they can toss out. These directories are good resources for inviting people to home parties and other sales presentations when you inform them that you're inviting your mutual group of friends.

> Use discretion and professionalism with this information so you're not looked upon as a scary solicitor.

To cover the cost of publishing directories, organizations often sell advertising. This could be a good use of your advertising budget because you already have a link with the people whose names are listed in the directory. Become familiar with the members of the groups and when your ad has your picture, the group will get to know you, especially when you meet in person at group functions.

✳ Displays

I recommend you mimic that proven retail marketing tool, the "Point of Purchase Display," but with a *TWIST*: Place a box with an advertisement about your business on the counters of businesses you frequent. Good choices are video stores, beauty salons, cleaners, copy shops, tanning salons—places with traffic and *thirsty* people! Every time you walk into a place of business, consider talking to the owner about this idea.

You can make your own box or purchase a display-style box at a local paper supplier. The box display could include flyers, coupon offers, product literature, and business cards. The key is to get the names and phone numbers of those who want to do business with you. Remember, people rarely call you, even if they want your product. Have a local printer supply you with note pads printed with spaces for name, phone, and/or e-mail address. Attach these pads to the box and provide a place for them to be deposited in the box. Do a drawing for products. Gather these leads often. Offer the business owner free products and referrals in exchange for letting you use some counter space. Or trade spaces with another business owner who wants to place his display box in your store or display.

> Check your lead boxes weekly and restock supplies.

One sales leader shared her experience with me about the time she saw a display box from her company at the local beauty salon. She asked the stylist for the name of the representative who had placed the box. The stylist replied, "Oh, that lady hasn't been back for weeks; I'm going to throw the box away." This smart leader told the stylist that she would take care of the box, and, upon opening it, found twelve leads. When she called the people, nine wanted to buy or sell her company's product.

The moral is: Maintain your display boxes by checking on them weekly while letting the owners/employees of the business know the box is valuable to you. It is!

If your product lends itself to a stand-alone display, check out venues which offer shelf space for rent and where you don't have to be on site. Some of these places encourage you to stock your shelves and when customers purchase the items, the

venue pays you after deducting a fee. This is a way to sell your products, but you're not meeting customers face to face, so you'll want to include a "Bounce Back" offer to entice them to call you. Also, don't keep a large stock of products as it might encourage theft. To find these places check out craft malls and antique malls on line.

✳ Distance Customers

Advanced, affordable delivery systems, coupled with inexpensive communications and technology, make selling around the globe easy and affordable (assuming you don't have to be licensed or are limited by geographical territory). Distance is no longer a limiting factor!

Contact people you already have relationships with who do not live in your area; those from places you used to live or people who previously lived in your city. Social networking websites like Facebook make this an adventure! Beyond relationships you've already established, promoting your business to people at a distance is best done by recommendations and referrals, on line or by purchasing demographically-targeted mailing lists.

(However, be wary of purchased lists: The data can be old! In fact, my husband occasionally receives promotional mailers addressed to an employer he lift nearly a decade ago!)

Create a challenge to find customers from as many states, provinces, or countries as possible. If you have a sales team or employees, include them. In this challenge, set milestones on the calendar and hang a map as a visual reminder. Reward yourself with a trip visiting your new customers in these new places. One of my consulting clients included a map of the United States in every monthly newsletter showing which states had representatives. This became a fun challenge to see how fast the company could grow across the country.

✳ Doctor/Dentist Offices

Who doesn't visit one of these offices a couple of times a year? Doctors and dentists are most often like you and me; they are business owners! They are

thirsty for customers! In fact, this book is a valuable resource for these professions, and because they own their own businesses, many are open to bartering.

A couple of years ago, I had my gall bladder removed. The balance due to the surgeon after my deductible was less than two hundred dollars. At the time, I was consulting for a client who allowed me to purchase products at wholesale. The product was unique and something that enhanced the décor and safety of the office. At my post-op appointment, I carried a basket with samples and after getting my clean bill of health, took a couple of minutes to show her what I knew could benefit her practice. She was impressed with the product and then excited to do business with me because I offered to barter. The two hundred I owed ended up costing me just over one hundred dollars after purchasing product from my client. My client loved this because his business now had a captive audience of my surgeon's patients. Triple win!

✳ Donations

Like most of the ideas in this book, donations can work two ways:

- ✳ Organizations can contact you to give to their cause
- ✳ You can contact organizations and offer to donate your product or service

Our company is often solicited to donate items for auctions, door prize drawings, bag stuffers for meetings, raffles and many other causes. I'm happy to donate through my donation budget. This means I set aside a dollar amount of inventory or service to give away when asked. After this annual amount is depleted, then the organizations can contact me the following year. I've yet to turn someone away, but I have a designated budget in the event requests out number resources.

When I give something away, I want everyone involved to benefit, so I request (insist) on something in return: The name and contact number or e-mail of the person who wins my donation. Here are a few ways to insure you make contact:

1. Donate services. This can be the best gift because while time is often more valuable than inventory, you are able to build a relationship with

the winner of your gift, which in turn can generate future business and referrals.

2. Award gift certificates rather than actual product so the winners can choose the size, color, or style of the item you're giving away. While I want the gift certificate to be for a free item, often a customer will use the certificate toward a larger purchase. When the winner contacts you, remember that this is a *gift*; while it's serviceable to recommend the gift can be used toward a larger purchase, don't give any indication that this is a condition of redemption. It is, after all, a *gift* certificate.

3. I've also discovered that many people are not as concerned about the gift they've won as they are to support the fund raiser. So, if they are required to contact you, the giver, they may simply give up the gift. In this case, I don't feel I've "thrown away" an unwanted service or product that was delivered at the event; I'd rather have a new contact *and* give something away. A worst case scenario is when the prize I've donated is unappreciated or tossed away because the winner was simply not *thirsty*. A gift certificate eliminates this type of waste.

4. Offer a free refill or bonus gift in addition to the base product that you're donating. Let's say your product is a home décor item. On the gift card (always attach a handwritten note of congratulations to the winner with your contact information, business card, and sales literature), announce that you'll add an extra picture, plate, lamp, etc. when they contact you within the next thirty days. This increases the value of the donation and the number of your customers.

Whichever method you choose, call the organization back after the event. First ask about the success of the event; be interested in their cause. If it didn't go as well as they hoped and they are still lacking funds, offer suggestions—perhaps your company or product—as a future fund raiser.

Next, ask for the contact information of the winner so that you can take the first step in getting to know them via a phone call, personal letter or e-mail.

The second way to donate is to approach clubs and organizations and give your product or service. This is a good way to reduce excess inventory, receive a possible tax deduction (do check with your tax advisor on this one), and find new customers.

Your benefit in using donations to find customers comes from giving the gift and then the possibility of receiving new business.

* Door-to-Door, Those You'd Like to Know

Decades before the Internet and years before the telephone was in every home, the prime way for a salesperson to meet new customers was to walk from door-to-door and visit face-to-face with prospects. As a sales professional for over thirty years, this has been one of the best ways to meet many committed customers. I recently read an article stating that, due to the Do Not Call List in the United States, many companies are hiring sales reps to go knock on doors and meet prospects. While many "No Soliciting" signs are now hanging on some doors, others are also welcoming visits from people like you.

Now that we are a more mobile yet more secretive society (we like our privacy; we don't want anyone, not even the neighbors knocking at our doors), promoting our business by walking door-to-door seems to be as outdated as film in a camera. Yet, as a consumer, I'm beginning to see more people visit my door to introduce themselves and their products.

A couple months ago, a husband and wife business couple walked through our neighborhood offering to paint our house number on the street curb for twenty dollars. They explained this aids emergency vehicles responding to calls. Within 15 minutes, our numbers were professionally posted on the curb and this team continued to walk through the neighborhood. Soon after, a lawn care professional knocked on my door advertising his company's service. I'm always impressed that business people and owners will do whatever it takes to find customers and so I like to support them as much as I can. Additionally, when I'm nice to people who come to my door, I know people will be kind to me, even if they're not *thirsty* for what I offer; I've haven't met a mean person or had a door closed in my face yet even though I've had my share of "nos."

We talk about one of the biggest benefits of shopping on line is that you don't have to *stand in line*. When a sales person knocks on your door, you don't have to travel anywhere, either.

Here are my tips and *TWIST*s about meeting customers in the comfort of their own homes.

1. **Dress to impress.** This does not mean suits and ties for men and skirts and heels for women. Clean, comfortable, and covered are the guidelines for dress in this case. A shirt or jacket with your company logo gives you instant identification as do credentials on a lanyard or a name tag.

2. **It's okay to carry samples** of products, but travel lightly with a small briefcase or basket; you don't want to look "salesy." If you find someone who is curious and will listen to you, be brief. Carry business cards or brochures in pockets or small purses or baskets and always have a small notebook and pen to record customers' or prospects' contact information.

3. **Identify the** *"thirsty-looking"* **homes**, when possible. One cool January day, I answered the ring of my doorbell and discovered a former neighbor, Brent, standing on my porch. Initially, I thought he was stopping by for an impromptu visit. He gave us a quick update on his family and then asked, "Have you noticed how bad the siding on the back of your house looks? It really needs a fresh coat of paint!" When our house was built seven years previously, Brent was contracted by our builder to paint several homes in our neighborhood, including ours, so he knew when the house had been originally painted.

   His question took me off guard; I rarely drove on the street behind our home, and the front and sides of our house are bricked so I was not aware of the condition of the back of the house. Further, prior to this home, we had never lived in a house longer than five years, so we weren't accustomed to long-term maintenance. He offered us his off-season rate with the confirmation he could begin the work immediately. We agreed and our house had a fresh paint job within a week. Ironically, one of our acquaintances was offended that we didn't hire his company to paint our house. But we didn't know that he had a home repair business on the side—he never came to our door or opened his mouth with an offer!

Years later, as we drive through our neighborhood and see many other homes that don't realize they are in dire need of new paint, I'm tempted to call Brent and have him knock on some of my neighbors' doors.

If your product or service cures a house that needs paint, a lawn that needs cutting, a fence that needs repairs, a car that needs a bath—a to name a few—go out and meet some new customers. These houses are crying for you!

On the other hand, you might own and operate a food distribution service. How can you tell if the occupants of a home are *thirsty* for your food? I like to choose friendly homes, those that look well-kept and welcoming with plants, flowers, and other seasonal decorations. One of my clients who began meeting new customers by going door-to-door reports she looks for "kiddie litter:" bikes in the driveway, toys on the lawn, mini van in the garage, to mention a few. Occupants of these homes could be *thirsty* for any family-related products or services.

4. **Get to the point.** Relationships are built on conversations, which take time; however, in this case, you're interrupting someone's day so if you want to make a friend, don't steal any more of their precious time. A quick introduction and then state your purpose: "Hi, I'm Robert with Super Clean Windows. Do you need someone to clean your second-story exterior windows so you don't fall and break your back?" Or, "Hello, I'm Deborah with Thread Designs (as she points to an embroidered shirt and purse she made); I create artistic designs on clothes, linens, or purses. Do you want to want to see some of my samples?"

5. **No begging allowed.** If the prospect says, "No thank you," or "I'm not interested," very kindly and sincerely thank them for opening their door to you and go on to the next door. Don't go on and on with a sales pitch! This is what gave the door-to-door salesperson a bad reputation. They're at a door with a captive audience and keep talking and begging until the homeowner slams the door!

6. **Timing.** There's never a good time and always a good time. You'll never find everyone at home! As you drive through a neighborhood watch for signs of life: cars in driveways, garage doors open, doors ajar, people going for walks, to mention a few.

7. **Walk with a friend.** When I teach this concept, many people are leery about the security of such an approach. I do not advocate taking any risks that would physically harm you, only those that will promote your business (a "no" is not harmful even if you think it is!). So, begin by working in your own neighborhood. Then choose neighborhoods where you think *thirsty* customers would live. Invite another consultant, sales rep, or new trainee to walk with you. Take turns talking and gathering leads. Or, divide and conquer as you each walk down one side of the street.

✳ Drawings

Drawings are intended to **draw** *thirsty* customers to you. If your business is a retail establishment or office where customers visit, offer drawings using a pre-printed form or the usual, "Drop Your Business Card" in the bowl drawing. Either option will capture information about your prospect.

> Position the choices so you're "taking temperatures" rather than asking for decisions.

Take drawings a step further and post pictures of the winners eating lunch at your restaurant, golfing at your golf course, showing their pearly whites after a free dental visit, making dinner with the free kitchen tools, or participating with whatever gift with which you've honored them. Invite them to submit a testimonial about using your product.

Don't neglect those who did not win the prize; this is where you find the *thirsty* customers. Contact them with another free offer such as buy one, get one free or send them coupons or gift certificates. If you gathered e-mail addresses and asked for permission to send offers electronically, this is the ideal way to communicate.

If you're a vendor at expos or events, drawings are a excellent method to award products to prospects as well as gather information to determine their level of thirst.

Pre-printed forms work well for consumer shows, while business cards are best for business-to-business events. The form should include their contact information: name, phone, e-mail, and address, although many folks are only willing to give e-mails. Make sure you leave plenty of room to write the information clearly.

The form can also list the services you offer where the prospect checks or circles his choices. Be careful not to ask for too much information, otherwise the forms are not filled out. Position the choices so you're "taking temperatures" rather than asking for decisions. Remember, your booth will be one of many hundreds they might visit, so you don't want to overwhelm anyone, including yourself.

To sift out those who have no *thirst*, I add an option at the bottom which says, "Call me only if I win." People chuckle when they read that one and feel safe in sharing their real opinions.

Add more value to the forms and take notes on their card or drawing slip as you visit with prospects. Many times, I'll say, "Let me jot that down and I'll remember to send you the details." By writing the details, prospects know I pay attention to details and they already feel confident in working with me.

✳ Drive-through windows

Drive more customers to your business when you drive through to pick up dry cleaning, make bank deposits, or pay for fast food. Surprise workers at drive-through windows by giving them an advertisement about your business. You can add literature, business cards, ad souvenirs (fun because they'll show these off to their co-workers), gift certificates, samples, or coupons to the drive through drawers!

✳ Elevators

Have you noticed how people act in elevators? They walk in, press the button for their floor, and then stare at the door, ceiling or floor. On the other hand, I love to make friends on an elevator, so as I climb aboard I announce, "I'll do the driving! Which floor do you want?" All of a sudden sullen faces smile as I start asking questions about them and group conversations begin. This is particularly great in hotels, where I happen to be staying for several nights. I might ask, "Are you coming or going?" "Where are you from?" "What brings you to this city?" There are all kinds of questions to ask about *them*. People love you to talk about their most important subject: themselves! I'm always amazed at what I learn on just a few of these "flights." If any of the "passengers" seem to be *thirsty* for my service or product, I exchange business cards with them. It's that simple!!

> Elevate your business and your interest in *thirsty* prospects when you ride an elevator!

One of the best elevator stories I've read was about a woman who owned a gift basket company and was looking for *thirsty* corporate clients. She carried samples of her baskets and rode the elevator in an office building. As people asked her what she was carrying, she explained her product and then gathered business cards and customers. Ingenious...a great example of the HOHO Lemon Aid Law for Locating Leads!

Perhaps you've heard "sales trainers" tell you to craft an elevator speech. Have you done this and do you use it? No? That's what I thought; I haven't either! Most people never use them because they are so contrived! Instead, do this *TWIST*, and if nothing else, the ice is broken, and the ride is more enjoyable!

✳ E-mail

Automatically attract *thirsty* customers every time you send e-mails for business or personal use by setting up a signature that will always be included in your e-mails. Look at the settings on your e-mail account and then incorporate these tips:

- ✳ Include your name and business
- ✳ Add a hyperlink to your website
- ✳ Include your phone number; some prospects would rather call you-very important yet seldom done
- ✳ Post a tag line, but don't overdo it with paragraphs of explanations and volumes of quotations. Keep it simple!

✳ Events, Expos, Exhibits

From high school craft fairs to coliseum expos, these events are becoming popular vehicles for capturing new business leads at a variety of venues for all types of audiences, and at various price levels. For over thirty years, I've exhibited in events from small, rural county fairs to huge metro events and continue to learn something new about how to attract customers at every event.

After one of my cross-country moves, I participated in a holiday craft fair in my new area. The leads I got from that one event were the catapult for huge business growth for years and years. In my consulting business, I advise clients with startup businesses to utilize this marketing channel. Some common denominators for success in all events are listed here.

Choosing an event: Pick one that will bring a target audience of *thirsty* prospects to you. For example, if you sell kitchen ware, going to a gun show would not be your most profitable choice; your *thirsty* audience would not necessarily be in attendance. A home and garden show or family fair would be a much better choice because it targets the folks who make up your target market. If you're a home-builder, a kitchen show could be a goldmine.

Who else will be there? Are other companies with the same product line going to be exhibitors? Is that okay with you? If my competitors are there, I generally want my presence there as well. Some events limit the number of participants in a particular category so it is not over represented. If you're an independent direct selling consultant, check to see if another consultant from your company has already registered. If the event is a huge state fair with multiple buildings, multiple booths representing the same company or product line could benefit everyone, as not every fair attendee goes to all buildings. Conversely, I've been to some events with fewer than fifty exhibitors and having duplicate representation from the same companies was not an advantage.

Booth Placement: Don't let the organizer randomly assign your space. Examine a map of the exposition before signing any contracts so you can know who the neighboring exhibitors are on both sides of your booth, across the aisle, and behind you. Consider what products they'll be marketing. Will the aroma of the food samples they give away draw people to your area? Will it compete with your food line, activity or product? Will the scents from your perfume irritate the travel agency next to you (I've experienced this one; it's not fun!).

Choose a space away from others selling the same or similar product. This is so that the visitors to your booth do not confuse you with someone else.

Try to get a high-traffic area; perhaps near the food court or restrooms, two places most visitors end up at some time.

I once exhibited at a bridal show and my booth was near the stage. At first I thought it would be distracting because of the on-stage events. The sound wasn't bad and in fact as the anticipated fashion shows started at three different times of the day, I was swarmed with visitors waiting for the show to start. You might pay a premium for better space, such as corners at the end of an aisle; you'll have to determine if it's worth it.

The Set up: Keep everything looking professional with well-designed signage; clean, solid-colored table skirts and coverings; and attractive displays. Some venues have professional decorating services. Always look your best in all ways as this is your introduction to new customers.

Keep the booth simple. Your product line might have hundreds of products, don't display them all because people will not take the time to sift through everything. You can always keep extra inventory stored under tables and behind curtains.

Open booths vs. closed: Make your booth inviting as if customers were coming into your store. My suggestion is a "U Shape" configuration which gives you three times more table space than if you put one table across the booth. You are paying for space; use it wisely! Many booths have the displays at the back of the booth, with the exhibitor in front behind a table, essentially blocking access to the booth. Potential customers don't get to see the products and the aisles then get crowded. You'll need to check the event contract to see what is and is not allowed.

Originality: The purpose of your participating in this event is to meet new customers and gather leads. The problem is that a hundred or more exhibitors are doing the same! So attendees are going to be bombarded with pitches and literature from every booth they visit. Make yours different.

At one event I participated in, a neighboring vendor drew large crowds because he offered to clean glasses and jewelry for free as a means of demonstrating his product. After the first day of this three-week event, I decided I needed to do something to attract more visitors. The venue was in downtown Dallas, Texas in July, with thousands of independent direct selling beauty cosmetic consultants. I knew they'd be *thirsty* for a cold drink *and* for my information. So we served cold lemonade in four-ounce cups—just a sip to quench their physical thirst. (Please note the synergy between this act and my personal icon, the Lemon Aid Lady.)

As the women walked by, I moved to the edge of my booth to get as close to the traffic as I could, and with an attractive tray filled with my cold lemonade I'd ask, "Are you *thirsty* (most would give the pasted-on smile and begin to say 'no thank you' while I kept asking the question) for more hosts, customers, and new consultants (exactly what direct selling people want)?" Wow! The end of that question grabbed them! They were in town to learn about building their business and I was there to quench that thirst! From that day on, our booth kept busy!

Be an active exhibitor: Many people staffing a booth just sit in their chairs, fold their arms and (some even have their noses in books) wait for people to come to their booth. The non-verbal message they send is "I don't really want to be here."

These are always the ones who whine that they're wasting time and money... and they are!

The key is to go out TO the people! Check your contract to see if you have limits as to where you can stand; some state that you must stay within your booth, which really protects everyone's territory. If this is the case, all you need to do is project your voice, and like I did with my tray of lemonade, walk out to the edge of the booth so visitors can hear—and see—you!

Put a dish of wrapped candy out to lure people to come over. Music or other multimedia (if allowed) attracts visitors as do cooking, crafting, or other demos if any of these are appropriate to your business.

Gather Prospect and Customer Information: While you want to sell product, your main objective is to gather information about prospective buyers. In fact, your relationship-based business depends on building relationships and this venue is the first step.

Your goal is to get names of new, potential customers. You must develop your own way of asking for this information that is perceived as a real benefit by the prospect. For many, prize drawings work wonders. Most people understand why you are doing this and are usually willing to fill out a slip. Make the forms simple to fill out—don't ask a lot of complicated questions! A prospect should be able to fill out the slip in less than 60 seconds. Clipboards with pens attached are a necessity in a booth for this very purpose.

After prospects give you their information, give them a sample of your product or a business card, literature, ad souvenir, or some small, inexpensive (yet valuable because your contact information is on it) item so they'll want to keep it and will remember you.

Show special for booth visitors: Have a great offer for "buy it now" customers. Many prospects will ask, "Do you have a website?" I know that often it's a way of saying, "I don't want to talk to you or buy from you right now." But you feel better because you think people will flock to your site and buy. Hardly! Some might, but most won't.

If you can announce, "Show Only Special" and mean it, then you'li have more sales because it's an impulse purchase. Be sure to get contact information with every transaction. If you receive a check for payment, there's no need to ask for phone and address as long as it's printed on the check. Simply verify the information is current, then ask for an e-mail address and, possibly, a driver's license number.

Just because someone doesn't want your product that very day doesn't mean they won't have interest or a referral when you call them back. I've found that some folks don't like lugging products around the events, and they actually prefer to be contacted later.

Other exhibitors: Get to know the other people manning booths. Use the ideas you're reading in this book to cross-promote, barter and reverse sell.

Follow through and you'll never be through! The most important key to any business is follow through! You can have the best-looking booth, capture hundreds of leads, but nothing, absolutely nothing works until you follow through!

> The fortune is
> in the
> follow through.

Enlist help; you'll be exhausted! These types of shows can drain more of your energy than running a marathon. If you have employees, assign them booth time with you. If you work in an office with other associates such as real estate or insurance agents, or have a direct selling or network marketing team, share booth time and expenses with them.

✳ Fast Food Places

If you're a parent, grandparent, or child care provider of any kind and frequently dine at fast food places with playgrounds, you could be sitting in the middle of *thirsty* prospects. When I take my grandkids to these venues, they end up making new acquaintances which essentially forces me to talk to the parents of those new-found buddies. This is a good opportunity to bring up your business.

> Many moms and dads who work from home or have lost a job are open to these conversations and opportunities.

Most parents exchange pleasantries, such as "How old is your child?" and that question leads to conversations. While a great place to discuss your business with anyone, this arena is particularly appropriate for direct selling consultants who not only have a product or service to sell, but also a business opportunity to explain.

If you want to have an informal display and demonstration of your products, put them on the table and go to work. Perhaps you have jars to label, beads to thread, or stickers to put on literature. People will approach you and ask what you're doing. It's a great way for people to experience your offering.

If you don't have a little one to play on the playground, take your lunch to that area and observe the parents (remember LLL and then BB). Naturally open up the conversation with compliments and commonality connections and you might find gallons of *thirsty* prospects!

❊ File Folders

My wonderful husband is a frequent file-er. No, I haven't misspelled that word, but there is not a word in the dictionary that means a person who files everything. Whenever a stray paper ends up on a desk, "Mr. Lemon Aid" files it! My problem is I forget what file I put papers in, so I simply create piles. The only difference between my piles and his files is that he labels his!

If you're a pile-er or a file-er you could have *thirsty* customers "hanging out" in your home or office. Here are some file types to check out:

❊ **Organizations** you are or have been a part of such as community clubs, churches, sports teams, or volunteer groups. In the files you could find rosters of names and phone numbers, programs with names of presenters or vendors, award certificates (who signed them?). These could be *thirsty* people for your business.

❊ **Vendors** who have or are currently servicing you. Remember when you had new kitchen cabinets installed and the salesperson and owner provided outstanding service? One, the other, or both could be *thirsty* to visit your new miniature golf course.

❊ **Past projects:** Perhaps you recently installed a sprinkling system and sod in your yard. You have a stack of business cards and job quotes with the names of sales people, account managers, and installers. After a long day at work, they might enjoy a free dessert at your new restaurant.

> Before you toss anything in the circular file, make sure you're not discarding potential customers.

❊ **School records:** These could be your own or your children's. Perhaps you "connected" with one of your kid's teachers two years ago because you grew up in the same state. She might be *thirsty* to visit your new furniture consignment store. If you were a student yourself, you might have files from all your classes, including the names of groups you worked with on assignments. Perhaps they'd all like to reconnect at a home event you're hosting to show the new stained concrete business you now own.

✳ **Customers**: If you've owned a business before or have been a sales representative previously, go through the files of people who already know you and your service qualities; they might just be *thirsty* to bring their cars to your new detail shop or hair salon.

✳ Flyers

Flyers can be an inexpensive "billboard" to advertise your business and can be distributed three ways:

Hang Up—in public areas such as bulletin boards, posts, or walls

Hand Out—in neighborhoods, at events, as an alternative to business cards

Send To—as self-mailers, in envelopes, or as "tip-ins" in newspapers or magazines

Creating the flyer: The secret to flyers, like billboards and printed ads, is to capture a prospect's attention within seconds. You begin with a catchy—yet targeted—headline and keep the rest of the text simple. Pay attention to magazine and newspaper advertisements. Which ones appeal to you? One of the most successful and often copied is the "Got Milk?" campaign. All kinds of businesses are asking prospects: Got _____? It's overused, but the simple question, added to two single syllable words pulls prospects in. Do a *TWIST* and use another verb:

Need Insurance?
Send Packages?
Use Electricity?
Play Tennis?
Watch TV?
Love Libraries?
Collect Clothes?
Want Windows?
Have Headaches?

Notice how the last four samples begin with the same letters of the alphabet; this is called alliteration. This is not necessary but makes the quick questions quirky. And easy to read...

One of my favorites to attract a very specific group of *thirsty* prospects is to ask for "lovers," "fans," "...holics" and other examples below:

Chocoholics Call:
Foodies Contact:
Antique Collectors Call:
Jewelry Divas Connect:
Camera Bugs Call:
Candle Fans Call:
Scrapbookers Contact:
Pizza Lovers Visit:

One of the most powerful words in the language is FREE. Use this in your head-lines:

Free Perfume
Free Pedicures
Free Furniture
Free Financing

The rest of the flyer invites them to call you or visit your website where you have more details. Adding an offer such as a coupon or sale notice, especially with a close expiration date, is a great way to encourage prospects to take action rather than to throw your flyer away.

Producing the flyer: Create flyers in a Microsoft Word document using large, legi-ble print and copy on bright, colorful, sturdy card stock. It's as simple as that. Unless you are an expert calligrapher or sign painter, don't handwrite the text; it looks amateurish in today's world of desktop publishing.

Now...

Hang up: These are the most difficult to get results from because you have to depend on your headline to catch a passer-by's attention enough read the flyer. But because the flyer is tacked to a wall, how will the prospect have your information other than writing down the details or punching it into a phone? You've probably seen posted flyers with the little sideways strips at the bottom that prospects can tear off. I've done that before and the strips are so small they end up in the bottom of my purse and collect dust and other objects! If I ever find the strips, all that's listed is a phone number and maybe a name. I don't remember why I have the strip, so I throw it away.

Here's the solution. Staple your business cards on the bottom of the flyer; one staple per card, please. If you turn the flyer so it's a *landscape* layout, you'll be able to include more cards. I suggest the cards are turned so the staple is on the shortest side. And you'll get more response if you have an offer on the back of your business card.

> Staple your business cards on the bottom of the flyer; one staple per card.

A fun *TWIST* is to create a promotional piece which is larger than a business card yet smaller than a flyer; I suggest a 4" x 6" postcard size. This can include a photo of your product with sales copy on the back, along with a great offer. Better than this is to create a collectible card with your photo and sales information on one side and something people will not throw away on the reverse. This could be a recipe, a poem, or a meaningful quote. People will collect and keep these! If you choose this idea, create a few different postcards for variety, but only hang all of the same so that you don't have a collector come and take all your cards.

Keep a supply of flyers in your purse or briefcase so you can hang them whenever you see a posted place. And flyers won't get folded and torn when you keep them in a file folder. Remember to have see-through thumb tacks for hanging as well as a stapler to attach the cards.

Hand Out: Flyers are more beneficial than business cards because you can include more details, like coupons and other offers. This is my choice for exhibits and events. If your children are older (pre-teen and teen) who want to earn money, hire them to deliver flyers in neighborhoods (do not let them be placed in mailboxes; it's against the law!) and pay them per flyer delivered with a bonus attached when the people they deliver to do become customers.

If you're going to host a product event such as a home presentation, I suggest delivering the flyers yourself so you can meet people face-to-face; they'll be more inclined to attend when they've met you.

Years ago, the owner of the fruit market in my little city walked through my neighborhood delivering flyers. I was impressed he took about an hour out of his day to meet the folks on our street. When I shopped at his store, we had a connection.

Send To: Create a mailer out of a flyer by leaving one of the panels blank when it's laid out. Not only does this save on envelopes, but prospects can immediately see your materials and then open the flyer. Check with your Post Office on mailing specifications. If you purchase mailing lists of prospects, flyers are a good way to introduce your business.

✳ Former Acquaintances

Think of people in your "former lives" including:

> Roommates
> Business Associates
> Customers
> Neighbors
> In-laws
> Co Workers
> Bosses
> Vendors

When you were closely associated with these folks, you probably knew a lot about their likes, dislikes, favorites, hobbies, and other personal data that could indicate they might be *thirsty* for your product or service. Let them know what you're up to as well as discover what's going on in their lives; most people are happy to reconnect after years of little or no communication as evidenced on popular social network sites like Facebook. In fact, that's a great place to begin to reconnect with people!

This has become a gold mine for connecting with friends and offering business opportunities because not only are you reconnected on line, you have a new

interest in common: the business. Perhaps they are looking for a company to be involved with—a great recruiting potential! If they don't need or want what you have to offer, ask for referrals.

✳ Friends

In the direct selling industry, consultants encourage their party plan guests to bring a friend to the party so they (the original guest) will receive a gift. This is a nice premise and way to award someone for a referral. The only problem is, the guest has no incentive to attend. So when I discovered this, I began awarding the guest *and* her friend the same gift!

I now offer this to my TelAdventure™ (presentations over the phone) attendees from time to time where they can bring a friend for free! That's a terrific value for everyone. My customer can bring a friend (it's up to her if she wants to charge her friend half of the fee she paid), a friend is taught great ideas, and I meet new customers!

But this technique isn't limited to direct sales: You can use it in any market! So, if you're a hair stylist, have a "Bring a Friend Day" for haircuts. Yes, you'll be working twice as much for the same fee, but now a new client has experienced your styling and service and will more likely to return. If the haircut is usually forty dollars, consider how impactful your advertising would be for that amount. Nothing!

If you're not able to do a "Friends-R-Free" promotion, consider a "Friends are Half" activity and see what the results are. The one stipulation I recommend is that the friends are people who have not done business with you previously. Be sure to capture the contact information for both the customer and the friend to follow up with a phone call, thank you note, or letter.

✳ Fund Raisers

Most non-profit organizations need to raise funds and look for unique ways and products to do so. Not only can your business be the sweet solution to their sour situation, but fund raisers can also be a wonderful way of finding and keeping more new customers.

What groups want: Leaders of these groups *do not* want the job of managing the fund raiser. So anything you can do to raise funds for the group without using the organization's resources— such as their employees and volunteers—the more the group will appreciate your efforts and use you as their vendor. When evaluating options, most decision makers look for a high profit percentage, as in fifty percent of sales. However, if your markup does not allow this, give a presentation to the decision-making committee and illustrate how your product can have more appeal, greater volume, and higher profits even at a lower percentage, if that is truly the case. Tell them that the Lemon Aid Lady says, "You can't spend percentages, only dollars!" In some instances, I've given up extra profits to pull up percentages because I consider a fund raiser an advertisement to customers. So, instead of paying for advertising, I was donating more dollars to my client and taking less profit, which in the end multiplies as more people use my products and continue as customers.

> You can only spend dollars, not percentages!

Finding fund raisers: The possibilities are everywhere! What groups are you a member of? Which church do you attend? What schools are your children enrolled in? Which sports teams do you or your children play on? What causes do you already support with cash or time donations? Do these bodies raise funds? If they've never done so, perhaps you can suggest getting started with your fund raiser program.

Watch for signs around your town, postings on bulletin boards, announcements in newspapers, and invitations to attend fund raising events. Support these fund raisers; get to know the organizer, and schedule an appointment for a presentation.

Approach and present: If you're a member of the group, you already have one foot in the door; people in the group know you so your trust and good service have been established. If you don't know the organizer and decision makers, contact them and ask for an appointment to present your program. If you purchased something from the organization previously, you'll be on common ground and able to ask, "How much money did you make from the bake sale?" Before you give the presentation, find out what purpose the funds are being raised for as well as what the funds have provided the group in the past. Bring samples of products or give services as a way to "test drive" the fund raiser.

TWIST on presentations: You are the expert regarding your product or service so create a very interesting presentation about the topic of your product or service and *volunteer* to be a no-fee speaker to the group. Let's say you own a pest control firm; you could create a presentation called "Quit Bugging Me" and approach various organizations with the offer to be a no-fee speaker at a meeting. As the group enjoys your information, they'll become *thirsty* to work with you. This is the perfect time to talk to them about a fund raising agreement.

> If you're a member of a group who needs to raise funds, you already have one foot in the door!

Be creative: We're all familiar with kids who come to our homes—or parents who bring flyers to work—for fund raisers as soon as the doors of the schools open in the fall. Products offered include: wrapping paper, greeting cards, candy bars, popcorn, even frozen cookie dough, among others. What kind of *TWIST* can you do to highlight your product and enhance the fund raising effort? If your service is the product, how can you position it as unique and memorable? Here are some ideas:

Restaurants: Allow the group members to be servers on a set time and date. All tips go to the organization. When the group announces this, the friends and family of the organization will fill your restaurant and you'll make more profits. Your regular servers might have to shadow and help the volunteers and you'll have to account for their compensation in some way.

Service Industry: If your service is carpet cleaning, you can give a percentage of the sales from a designated time period for appointments scheduled through the organization's name. This is best done in a short window of time during a typically slow season of your business: if you own a chimney cleaning service and autumn is your rush period, offer the fund raiser in early spring when people don't think of their chimneys.

Perpetual Fund Raiser: Establish a long-term association with a group, and agree that any referrals for a lengthy amount of time will be given cash referral rewards to the organization. For instance, if you own a dry cleaning establishment and members of the group and people they've referred bring their cleaning to you, the

transaction is recorded as a fund raiser referral and each month for a period of 12 months this amount is donated to the group. If you use this approach, ask if the organization has publications and websites where this can be announced each month. You should not need to pay for the advertisement because it's promoting a fund raising opportunity...and your business.

Involve the group from the beginning: The more members of an organization who are involved and aware of the fund raiser, the greater the sales to you and profits to the group. This is accomplished with a kick-off meeting, which in itself needs plenty of publicity to encourage a large crowd. At this event, you'll have literature or packets prepared for those who want to participate; include a *simple* letter of explanation.

Take advantage of any types of communication sent to the group members such as newsletters, posters, e-mail blasts, and banners. Entice attendance with free samples or advertising souvenirs, if available and appropriate. A raffle of your product or service will usually cover the cost of the product and other promotions, and excites people when they see themselves winning the prize. Come to an agreement with the group leaders that the raffle funds are to be used to cover this cost rather than to go into their coffers. As the group understands how the product works and has an *experience* rather than simply an *explanation,* they'll begin to open their mouths and raise funds!

> Entice attendance with free samples or advertising souvenirs, if available and appropriate.

Have the organization decide on a goal—how much do they want to earn? What will the money be used for? How much needs to be sold to meet this goal? How many average-size orders will be needed to sell this much product? Now, both you and the organization have goals clearly defined. Announce this at the kick off, continue to remind group members of this focus, and keep them appraised of the progress as sales are turned in.

Include a letter of explanation to those who will be gathering orders. Make this letter simple!

Contests: Speaking of prizes...people love promotions. Promotions are the stimulus that opens the mouths of the participants. Of course, you'll want to reward

those with the greatest dollar amount of sales as well as the highest number of orders. Competitive folks eat this up, but if you only award the "toppers" you're missing out on orders. Whenever possible, use your product as an incentive to get more and bigger orders. Establish levels of sales where you'll award movie passes, fast food gift cards, or other items appropriate to the audience. Of course, you'll need to factor in the cost of the gifts when presenting your percentages. Barter with other businesses for gifts to give participants a variety.

Processes: If you sell a large line of items, choose only a few for the fund raiser because you've got to make it simple to order. The object is to raise funds, not create chaos and headaches!

If you're required to collect sales tax, include it in the price so customers don't have to do any figuring; same for any shipping or handling fees. Somewhere on the literature, give instructions to whom the check needs to be payable. Will you accept credit cards? If so, how will you do this so the number remains safe? Always ask for names, phone, address, and e-mail so the product can be delivered easily and you can follow up on your service; this is the way you'll be nurturing new customers.

> Always ask for names, phone, address, and e-mail so the product can be delivered easily and you can follow up on your service; this is the way you'll be nurturing customers.

❋ Garage Sales

Garage sales are not much different than exhibiting at an event because, while the main intention is to buy or sell unwanted items, you can also be meeting new customers, perhaps in your own neighborhood. If you don't want to go to all the work of holding a garage sale of your own, do the *TWIST* and benefit from visiting with people who are holding garage sales.

Visiting garage sales—individual homes: Read the paper for garage sale listings in your area. Can the home owners use something of yours for free or a low fee, like a cabana with your company's logo on it? If you're a printer, print "Garage Sale" signs with your logo at the bottom, or create an entire Garage Sale kit and make it available for a nominal fee. If you have a food delivery service, drive around to the garage sales and offer to take orders, and then deliver the meals to these hard working people. Are you starting a business involving the creation and distribution of a special food recipe? Begin by selling the goods at garage sales first to get feedback on the taste and price; keep in mind that garage sale shoppers are looking for bargains.

> Add listings of garage sales on your website at no charge.

Neighborhood or group events—sponsoring: Offer to sponsor the event by paying for all or part of the newspaper advertising, where your logo will be displayed and you'll be listed as a sponsor. Donate bags from your store for the treasures guests will purchase and include coupons or gift certificates for *your* products or services. If you're a food vendor, bring your truck or set up an area to sell

refreshments, especially cold beverages. Allow the group to hang notices about the sale in your office or retail store.

Neighborhood or group events—observing: You can find out a lot about people by seeing what kinds of things they are getting rid of. If you see exercise equipment on the driveway with a "For Sale" sign, ask the owner if it works. She may reply, "It does, but I don't." She might lament that exercising hurts her knees. So if you're a physical therapist, maybe you can quickly show her the correct way to stand on the machine. You might even teach other shoppers some hints on the proper use of exercise equipment! Not only will your new acquaintance reconsider selling the machine, she'll be grateful for the knowledge you shared. Inform her of your services, get her number so you can keep in touch and perhaps gain a new patient.

> You can find out a lot about people by seeing what kinds of things they are getting rid of.

Remember that people are at garage sales looking for bargains; they will probably not want to purchase new items at a retail price. Giving your business exposure for future contacts is the goal here.

Many times garage sales will be held by groups to raise money. Approach the group after the sale to see if they want to hold a fund raiser with your company.

While garage sales are organized to clear out one person's junk to become another's treasure, many are held because the homeowner is moving, liquidating an estate, needing cash, or transitioning to another phase of life. If your product is the sweet solution for one of these needs, you could find more customers by visiting with the home owner. Case in point: If you're a real estate agent and discover the homeowner is getting rid of stuff so the house can be placed on the market, you could become the listing agent. Or, if the homeowner states she lost her job and needs cash from the sale, and you're a representative for a company who offers a business opportunity, you might have found a new sales consultant.

Hold your own garage sale: This is a great way to meet new customers, although it requires a lot of preparation. Along with items you want to rid your home or office of, you can also have a display of new products or services in a separate area so they are not confused with your junk/your visitor's treasures.

If your business allows you to regularly update items in your home or office—leaving you with an abundance of things you no longer need—garage sales give you opportunities to find *thirsty* people to buy your excess. For instance, if you recently opened an interior design service and retail store, you'll want to have the nicest, newest, products in your home. So sell your old wall hangings and accent pieces. Those who buy these items are *thirsty* to have their home looking nice, and when you meet them and explain your services, they could become your newest clients.

Drawings and give aways: If you have a fun advertising souvenir, give one to each *thirsty* visitor. Just as you would hold a drawing to gather contact information from prospects at an expo or event, do the same at your garage sale. Display a group of products or hang signage announcing the drawing and while shoppers are checking out their garage sale finds, they can be a step closer to being a customer or client.

✳ Gift Certificates and Gift Cards

Gift Certificates issued by you have a high perceived value and until they are redeemed by customers and prospects, the only cost to you is the printing. Value is created when more senses are involved; in this case, holding a hard copy printed by you or downloaded by a customer. Gift cards can be designed with your logo and are another value-added point. Here are some ideas for this valuable tool to attract more customers to your business:

1. Use in place of coupons. Coupons convey a cheap bargain; gift certificates add a touch of class and represent real value. These can be printed in ads or on flyers and you can send them to customers as a "Thanks for doing business," or "Congratulations on your achievement."

2. Gift certificates can be used to create a *thirst* for new business by sending them to prospects, perhaps those who entered your drawings for a free lunch, or a contest drawing at an expo event. In these cases, I suggest a gift certificate attached to a minimum purchase. For example, a $5.00 gift certificate with the purchase of $25.00. Of

course, you need to match these numbers with your price point and profit margins.

3. Gift certificates become a "create your own special" promotion when you accept them for any item or service. Consider specifying a product category, such as $5.00 gift certificate toward any gallon of paint.

4. Enclose gift certificates in your mailing pieces and greeting cards.

5. Use them as drawing gifts when giving fee-based or free presentations.

6. When donating product to fund raising events, consider giving gift certificates so that the recipient needs to contact you to get the gift. This allows you to provide great service as you guide the winner in choosing which item(s) are best for them. This is the essence of finding more customers with gift certificates. Because if you just hand over product at these events, you won't always get the name of the winner. And what is also unfortunate, is the product you donate might not be used and appreciated by the winner because he didn't choose it initially.

7. Staple them to the bottom of your *Hang Up Flyers.*

8. Hand them to cashiers, sales persons, and other great providers who service you.

9. Always post a general expiration date such as, "Please redeem within 30 days." You don't know when the prospect will be *thirsty* to use the gift certificate and while you want to create a feeling of action and urgency, you also don't want them to toss out their "ticket" to do business with you because they think it's too late.

10. Selling gift certificates can be the answer to gift giving dilemmas. In this case, you might not be allowed by law to post an expiration date because the certificate has been purchased; you have already received payment and now need to provide the product on demand. When people purchase gift certificates, you can offer to add the recipient's name to a mailing list or electronic newsletter so you can encourage her to redeem it.

11. When selling gift certificates, give an additional bonus: a gift certificate for a specific product or incentive when the certificate is redeemed by a specified date; this encourages rapid redemption. Here's a scenario: Joseph buys a gift certificate from your tire shop in

the amount of fifty dollars for his son's birthday. You advertise a "matching gift" which is a gift certificate for a half-price oil change. Joseph's son now has two reasons to use both gifts and to become a committed customer.

✳ Gift Giving

Whenever any gift-giving occasion arises, think of your product first as an appropriate gift. Not only can you give a nicer gift because you buy the product at wholesale cost, but the recipient becomes acquainted with your product. Include your business card as well as any other sales literature with the gift so the recipient knows how to use the product, learns how to make an exchange, or has information for future orders.

If you use your product at group gift giving occasions such as birthday parties and showers, other guests will be introduced to your company and many will inquire about how they can also make a purchase.

> Print a separate business card that reads "Corporate Gift Giving Specialist."

Teachers: One of my friends swears that the reason her kids got good grades is because she gave their school teachers products from her business for every holiday and other gift-giving occasions! This is a thoughtful gesture and also expands your business because other teachers see the gift ideas and will want to purchase items from you. They identify you with your product line, and this is also a great way to introduce your product as a potential fund raiser.

Corporations spend thousands of dollars on gifts for their employees, vendors, and customers. How could you promote your product to be their gift of choice? While these companies are usually conscious of price, the service is what will make the biggest difference to them. Let them know how you can serve them. If you can give a corporate or volume discount, you may be able to secure the business even easier.

Advertise this service by having a separate business card printed that reads "Corporate Gift Giving Specialist." When you meet people on a professional level, give them this card rather than your regular one.

Customize gifts with the company's logo. I offer this service with my CookINspiration company where I create recipes and messages specific to the giving client. It's a gift people keep for years.

Gift Certificates and gift cards can be specially designed for clients' gift giving needs. Be creative by adding a unique holder for the cards.

Greeting Cards

When you receive a greeting card in the mail, you know it's not a bill or an advertisement because it's "packaged" in a different-sized (and perhaps colored) envelope without a see-through window! And, it's usually hand addressed. To attract more customers, you should *market* with greeting cards rather than typical advertising. Think about it: every day of life should be a celebration, so why not create a celebration and mail a matching card to prospects. Custom cards can be printed rather inexpensively.

> Market with greeting cards rather than typical advertising.

Traditional uses of greeting cards such as thank you notes, recognition, or celebrations—even without any type of marketing—will keep your name in your prospect's mind; the grateful part, which has the best memory.

❈ Grocery Stores

Joint ventures: Next time you walk into a grocery store, look at all the examples of joint ventures: fast food restaurants, banks, photographers, video vendors, shoe stores and more are sharing space at your local grocers. Yes, these businesses pay for the real estate. However, I've seen many small businesses showing their wares in the aisles for free or for a low fee, from local clubs selling baked goods to newspapers signing up subscribers. How could your business bring customers to both the grocer and your company?

A well known, national baby store contacted me to set up a table in their stores throughout the Dallas, Texas area. My client's product did not compete with any of

their lines yet their clientele was very *thirsty* for what I was asked to display. Great leads were found and relationships established even though sales transactions were not allowed.

Yours, mine, ours: Demonstrate products from the store and yours together so both can be sold in tandem. One of my companies, CookINspiration™, attracts new customers best when I demonstrate recipes. I can work with grocery stores to feature their products while teaching customers a recipe and sharing an inspirational message.

Paid advertising opportunities: Shopping cart, register tape, and divider bars advertising are available media to attract customers at a price. You'll have to decide if it's worth the investment.

HOHO: Hang out in the area where your product could be on the shelf to survey and to look for new customers in a professional way. Remember, they're there to shop, and you don't want to steal business, yet if you overhear conversations and realize the customer is stumped to find the solution that you can offer with your product, open your mouth.

Years after I resigned my position with Tupperware, I was shopping at the grocery store for paper towels. In that paper and plastics supply aisle, I overheard a lady say to her son, "Find the Tupperware bowls for me." I'd been with the company long enough to know they did not have presence in that grocery store, so I approached the customer and explained if she wanted the real thing, she'd need to work with a sales consultant. She gladly gave me her name and contact number and I called the local office to pass the lead along.

Tag—you could be it: If you have a name tag identifying your company and position, always wear it when you're working or even if you're not as long as *you're dressed to do business*. Name tags attract attention. If someone is *thirsty* for your product and sees your name tag identification, they'll approach you. What a simple way to attract new customers!

Here's a **TWIST**: Watch for other people wearing name tags. Could they be your *thirsty* audience for bartering, cross-promoting, or as a customer? Be bold and begin a conversation.

Go Green: Recyclable shopping bags with an imprint of your company logo are inexpensive. Use your bags while you're shopping and your business will get exposure. You can also offer them as a complimentary gift to people in front and behind you in the checkout lane. Gauge their *thirsty* temperature and ask them for their contact information for future follow through.

The Foyer: This is the part of the store that has the Community Bulletin Board. Be prepared to hang a flyer; keep a supply of thumb tacks, tape, and stapler in your purse/briefcase/product bag so you'll have the tools to post it. While you're doing this, take a minute to look at those already posted. Remember, use the reverse selling *TWIST* and ask yourself, "Who on the board has a business or service that could benefit from my business/service? Anyone you'd like to barter with? How about possible cross-promotions?

> Always, always, always read the bulletin boards to get new leads.

Line up the leads: The most dreaded part of the shopping experience can become very profitable in the way of meeting new people while you're standing in line. You'll now see, you want to be in a lengthy line so you can linger longer and meet new leads!

Observe the people around you and look at what's in their grocery cart. If you see a man buying stacks of frozen dinners, you MIGHT surmise (but do not assume!) that he is single. You could open the conversation with a complimentary statement and lead in with questions: "Looks like you're a great cook!"

His response will determine how you'll take the conversation. Some people are tight-lipped and don't want to visit with anyone. Respect them. However, I've found that most people like to while away the time standing in line and open up. He might reply, "My wife is out of town this week." Well, now you know he isn't single. If your product is nutritional supplements, this is a great opportunity to briefly explain what you do and what you market.

I always tell people, "This is your lucky day, (every time someone meets me, they're lucky; and I'm lucky for having met them as well!) I just discovered some nutritional supplements that will add value to the foods you already eat."

If you are a female, males sometimes shy away. If you know they are married, (or you can outright ask if they are), ask for his wife's name. And, if you're male, this works by asking a woman for her husband's name. Spouses always seem willing to give their partner's name out.

Cash in with cashiers: Once you've made your way to the check stand, you now have a new prospect, the cashier! In most cases, they'll say something trite like, "Hi, how are you today?" Respond by using their name (look at the name tag). "I'm wonderful, Amy (use the right name), how are you doing?" A person's name is the sweetest word to them. Get to know the checker in much the same way as I've suggested that you talk with customers by asking questions about them!

If your business is marketing shoes with springy soles, the cashier could be a very *thirsty* prospect because she stands on her feet for hours on end. Or, if you have a business opportunity with a network marketing or direct sales company, and the cashier indicates she's tired of working for someone else, you now have a *thirsty* lead. Say something like, "Amy, you must really like your job" (always assume that she does, but usually the response is negative). Weave a few quick facts about your company into your conversation then ask for her business card (which she probably doesn't have) or her contact information so you can follow through.

> Always gather contact information so you can follow through to nurture the leads.

After you pay for your groceries, thank the cashier for the great service and say, "In appreciation of your great service, I have a gift for you." The gift is something with your contact information and business advertisement that she'll want to keep, such as an advertising souvenir, catalog or other literature. Remember to ask for her contact information so you can follow through!

Another idea along the same lines: have an offer printed up on business card-sized cards. You can put this either on the windshield or on the handle of the door. This is smaller and less bulky than regular flyers. People collect business cards and could be more inclined to read and keep something on this format.

❋ Halloween

When the trick-or-treaters come to your door, in addition to handing out treats, give them some literature and/or samples of your product in their bag with a note to the parents. Put your name and phone number on everything and add an offer with a gift certificate attached to a simple note saying, "A Treat for Mom (or Dad)." Of course, if the treat is a chocolate bar, the parents will be thrilled!

If the parents walk up to the door with the kids (or if you see them waiting on the sidewalk), hand the treat directly to them or invite them to come to the door so they identify you with the treat.

Many communities have trick or treating events where the goblins visit retail establishments. Open your store to this opportunity and you'll be opening doors to more customers, literally.

During the Halloween season, carry a treat bag or plastic pumpkin filled with treats to give potential customers, and tape your business card to the treat; exchange your treat for their contact information. Not only are you giving something tasty and tangible away, you're drawing attention to yourself and your business in a fun, non-threatening way. The treat does not always have to be something you eat. Advertising souvenirs work great because they become a keepsake.

✳ Handouts

Hand prospects valuable information and they'll keep it!

At Presentations: If you're giving a free or fee-based presentation to groups always include complimentary handouts with your information. This is particularly important if you're not selling your product or service, so that the audience will have something to keep and possibly do business with you after the event. Place your contact information on the bottom of every page of the handout, in addition to posting it on the cover.

> Handouts are valuable documents and a way to stay in contact.

I recently attended a wonderful, four-day event sponsored by one of my mentors. He invited other business owners to give presentations applicable to the topic of the conference, and of course, each had a product or service to promote (which I enjoyed because I accumulate a base of possible providers). Over the four days, at least eight different business owners shared their knowledge and then gave a pitch for their conference offer. However, only the last presenter had a professionally designed, information-packed handout along with his company name and contact information at the bottom of every page.

The handout was an active part of the talk because the presenter referred to each page as we took notes and filled in blanks. The handout became a valuable document for me to keep.

Of all the presenters over that four-day event, he was the one I chose to work with on future projects. I made the investment that day. Was it only because of his handout? No, he had great information as well. However, if I now wanted to contact one of the other speakers from that weekend, I'd have to spend time looking for their contact information as the only things they gave me were promotional materials, most of which were pitched when I returned home.

Quick Tip Sheets: In place of a business card, give a handout listing tips to enhance the prospect's life. For instance, if you're a music teacher, hand out a card listing the top five ways to encourage children to practice music. If you're a massage therapist, hand out tips on reducing stress in the workplace. The tips should coincide with your service and include your contact information.

✳ Headlines

Use very simple, catchy headlines to attract attention and encourage immediate action.

When a potential customer reads any of your literature, your goal is to have them respond quickly! If they have to muddle through pages of information, they put it aside until they have time, which is usually never. Use very simple, catchy headlines to attract attention and encourage immediate action. If you're not skilled at thinking up headlines, do a *TWIST*. Read and observe literature that you get from other businesses. How could you incorporate new ideas into your business? Read lots of magazines and open and read your junk mail (it's actually jewel mail!); they are full of great ideas and headlines!

Here are some very simple ones I've seen and used:

"Don't Throw Me Out"
"Give me Away"
"Read This"
"Pass me On"
"Need _____?" (Money, Time, Energy, etc)
"Are you looking for_____?" (New job, happiness, peace,)
"Are you confused about_____?" (insurance, legal advice,)

Adapt these headlines to the needs of your customers and the benefits you can offer.

✳ Health Clubs

You can grow a *healthy* business while you're working on your own physical fitness. Always wear workout clothes with your company's logo. If you're running on a treadmill next to other people, they might be watching the TVs suspended from the ceiling or listening to music on their mp3 players; but they'll see the reflection of your logo in the mirror during the entire workout session. If you don't have clothes with your logo, use health-related advertising souvenirs like pedometers, sweatbands, or water bottles and then give these out to other members of the club.

After taking a water aerobics class one morning, I was doing my hair and makeup in the dressing room of the health club. I had all my equipment in a duffel bag with my company's logo. A lady standing next to me saw my bag and asked if I was affiliated with the company. Upon my affirmation, she asked if she could host a sales demonstration with me. Her demonstration (first of many she held with me) sold over $1,000 worth of product and several people scheduled their own presentations from that one. I made thousands of dollars and gained hundreds of new customers just from carrying that bag.

> Vary the days and times you work out so you meet different groups of people.

Because you are in a causal atmosphere and tend to see the same people time after time, people might ask questions about your product. You should also vary the days and times you work out so you meet different groups of people.

Obviously, this is great venue if your product/service is health related. Perhaps you can place a small display of your products in the club or hang flyers or advertisements.

* Home Builder Shows

Most communities have a parade of homes program where builders construct showcase homes in one neighborhood (or scattered around the city) and sell tickets to allow the public to tour these decorated houses. Additionally, some shows have an exhibit tent set up so prospects can meet vendors. Would you like to be one of these vendors? The exhibit fees can be high and the events lengthy—many times over the period of a week or more. Consider these factors when making your decision to participate.

My preference is to have a display in one of the homes. Contact the home builders association and find out when the event is held. Get names of participating builders and ask if their home is a "builder-spec" home or if someone has already purchased it. If the builder owns the home, work directly with him. This can be a great opportunity for some cross promoting. Otherwise, contact the owners to make arrangements with them.

I've worked directly with home owners. Typically I was able to get them really excited about having my product in their new house. I'd then propose setting up a display in the area of the home where the items would be used. Brochures, catalogs, order forms, drawing slips, and perhaps samples were included.

> My preference is to have a display in one of the homes; it's less costly in both money and time.

The great thing about this approach is you can choose how long you will be on site, unlike being in the exhibit tent. On particularly busy days, such as weekends, stay at the home to answer questions and visit with *thirsty* customers. Other than that, just stop by daily to freshen up the display, restock supplies, and gather filled-out drawing slips.

If your company is based on the home party concept, or if you decide to use this great marketing channel, schedule a home demonstration with the owners after the builder expo so they can show off the home to their friends and family. Use this event to educate and service guests on your product and service. Give the homeowners any credit for the referrals and sales gained from the home demonstration as well as from the show display. Every time I participated with homeowners in this way, they became very loyal customers.

❋ Home Owners Associations

Many planned developments have home owners associations, which can introduce you to groups of *thirsty* prospects and customers. Are you a member of one of these? If so, begin with your own association first and then expand to others.

Newsletter Advertising: The newsletter, either hard copy or electronic, might be a great vehicle for advertising because you could have a highly targeted, *thirsty* audience, depending on the demographics of the development. The cost is usually very affordable (it could be free with your own association), and because the audience is smaller than that for newspapers or magazines, it's more personalized. As in any advertising, you'll want to be a "regular" in every issue. Remember people need to be introduced to a new concept over eight times before they decide to take action.

Newsletter Column: The volunteers who put the newsletter together are always looking for interesting content. Offer to write an article for every issue based on your business and at the same time focused on the property owners. Let's say you own a pest control company; your column could be titled "Bugs Be Gone." For each issue, you write a fun, humorous column about a pest in your area and how to tell if that pest has created a nest in a home. When the residents do identify that pests have joined their family, they'll know who to call first—you!

Directory of Residents: Some associations print hard copies of directories annually, or post them on line. If your association has not done this, volunteer to compile one. Most homeowners must give their permission to have this information shared, so you'll be contacting everyone and will get to know them. Many association directories include advertising from local merchants; here's another usually affordable medium where you'll want to list your business. When you have a directory of all the home owners, you can do some follow through by phoning or sending your own direct mail pieces to enhance the newsletter and directory advertising.

Celebrations: These events can be socials throughout the year, such as block parties or holiday get-togethers, when you have an opportunity to visit with your neighbors. You can offer to sponsor a part of the celebration, from the DJ to the paper supplies to goody bags, all of which can list your company name.

Clubs: One association we were members of had so many clubs that you could go to a different activity every day of the week! This was because we had over a thousand homes in the development, which meant a lot of people with different interests. Clubs are a fun way to get to know neighbors and for them to get to know you. As they do, you'll become their friend and a possible business supplier.

> Write a regular column for the association newsletter or sponsor an event.

Business Expos: This is an opportunity where businesses set up booths at the club house or other venue and invite both residents of the city and of the development to participate. If an association does not offer business expos, suggest it. The ones I've participated in charge a very nominal fee for a table; thus, if the association acts on your suggestion, it'll have another source of revenue which can reduce annual fees, so the residents are happy!

Some associations limit their advertising, events, and expos to residents only (very unfortunate for everyone!). If this is the case, you'll want to recruit or employ someone from each development quickly! And, even if you find this is the policy, you can still ask if it can be changed. Money talks, and many associations like to have the money in their coffers for the upkeep of their facilities.

Fund Raisers: Speaking of upkeep, if you find that the association is looking for additional funds, offer a fund raiser. This is a great way to get into the area and meet the residents.

Volunteer: Every association I've been a member of is always looking for residents to fill positions on the board or on committees. Not only is this a way to serve your community, but it's also an opportunity for people to get to know you and identify you with your business. If you're appointed or elected to one of these offices, always add your business name and position on your profile that's listed on the association website or literature. Business owners, sales persons, and company leaders have a lot of credibility with residents because it's implied that these people have managerial skills and networking talents that are critical to the positions.

✳ Home Presentations and Parties

The concept of selling products with groups of people (mostly women) in a home setting began over sixty years ago and has only grown stronger as a marketing channel. Pioneers in the industry range from Stanley Home Parties to Tupperware, Mary Kay and The Pampered Chef. Today, there are literally hundreds of companies that have adopted this plan. Over the past thirty years, this is the industry I've worked in as an independent sales consultant and leader as well as a business marketing consultant, where I develop sales education, leadership and marketing programs. If you are an independent consultant for one of these hundreds of companies, you'll want to check out my complete line of products and services for the direct sales industry at www.LemonAidLady.com

However, home presentations and parties are not limited only to the direct selling industry where host gifts and recruiting are an added ingredient to the selling of products.

Smart companies are now recruiting hosts for one-time-only launches of new products. For example, if a pizza restaurant wants to introduce a new recipe, they'll recruit, through an on line interview process, hosts to open their homes on a specific day with very detailed instructions on organizing the party. There are no demonstrators as in a typical home party or sales to be made. Instead, products are sampled and coupons and other incentives are given to the guests for future purchases. Home parties have become a low-key way to pull targeted audiences together to sample new products.

> The home party concept can be adapted to many industries and can be very powerful and profitable!

Additionally, because of my expertise in developing home party plans, I've had companies approach me to develop a home sales pitch for replacement windows, home electronics systems, and real estate. Home parties are one of the best ways to reach out and find new customers. Keep in mind these non-traditional home parties can initially take a lot of planning and preparation, and the key is to find a very *thirsty*, targeted audience for your product. However, by making this a fun, educational event, guests will want to bring their *thirsty* friends, making the party even more powerful and profitable!

❊ Honorary Days

One afternoon a flyer was placed on my door by a local pizza restaurant with a great offer: our street had been chosen for the daily promotion. The offer was only good that day, and I accepted; we had pizza for dinner that night!

What *thirsty* group could you honor with a special day? Announce your honorary days on marquees outside of your business, on your website, and in print, radio, or TV ads. You might want to designate your usually slowest day of the week to be an "honorary day". For example, announce to your customers that every Wednesday will be an honorary day and to check your website weekly to see if you are honoring their group. Here are a few ideas (you can ask for proof that they really are part of the group that you are honoring):

❊ Families of service men and women who are currently deployed
❊ Parents who home school their children

- Persons older than 30 who have returned to college
- Coaches of little league sports teams

The groups you honor should be a market you've identified as *thirsty* for your product.

Hotels

When you check into a hotel, offer to leave a basket of samples or advertising souvenirs at the front desk as a welcome gift for travelers, especially if these items are something travelers are *thirsty* for, such as luggage tags, key rings, or sewing and first aid kits.

You can also ask the front desk employees if you can leave a product on the table in the lobby or breakfast area. One of my clients sold a product with a unique alternative to flame-burning candles. When I checked into hotels, I'd offer to place one of the scent lamps on a table in the lobby next to which I put company catalogs. The scent drew the guests to the source and they picked up a catalog; I later received calls about the product!

> Leave a product catalog on the pillow along with a tip for the housekeepers.

I did some informal marketing surveys during breakfast at a casual, family-style hotel while working with a client who was in the process of renaming and branding the core product. During breakfast, I had the product on the table with my laptop turned on as if I were working (which I was). As I noticed people finishing their breakfast and leisurely sipping their coffee (I don't interrupt people who appear to be rushing, are engaged in conversations, immersed in reading the newspaper or attentively watching the news) I inquired, "Do you have a quick minute to give your opinion on something?" I showed the product and said, "We're naming this product; which name do you think best describes it?" While I really did want to know their opinion, several were curious enough to ask me more about how they could own this item.

What do *you* want to test? While you're taking a rest at a hotel, you just might discover some *thirsty* prospects.

You probably carry a laptop when you travel, but each time you're at a hotel, go to the business center to log onto the Internet. Visit your own website and leave the computer on your home page. The next person who uses the computer will see your site first and could be your next *thirsty* customer!

When I work with clients to set up product launches, sales meetings, or informational opportunity events, I personally call the hotel sales department to secure meeting space. When I identify myself and my client's company, I'm usually asked about the client; it then offers an opportunity to explain what the product or opportunity is all about. I make a point to bring a product gift to the sales manager with whom I'm working, and if possible, samples or souvenirs for the sales staff. Depending on the circumstance, I invite the employees to stop by during our meeting or event to learn more.

> Visit your own website on the public computer in the business center and keep your home page open for the next user to view.

There are times I research hotels for future meetings, but don't choose a particular one. However, I'll stop by and meet the employees at that property if I have time while I'm in the area, or send them product or opportunity information. I explain that another location was chosen, but that I want to keep in touch for future events. Not only do I begin a relationship for other company meetings, but I also introduce new customers to products, services, and opportunities they would not have heard otherwise.

When you leave your room for the housekeeping staff, leave the customary tip AND some literature, samples, and a gift certificate. A sincere thank you note is appreciated when appropriate (for good service). Hotel housekeeping is not the highest paying job, so these people might be candidates to become new members of your team if you're looking for new sales reps.

Even if no business is generated, you are giving another person a sincere compliment; someone who normally does not get written praise from the public. You also give a great impression of you and your company!

Hotel lobbies have become leisurely meeting places. One day I was sitting in the lobby waiting for my ride and I met several *thirsty* prospects while I listened to conversations at the front desk as people were checking in and out of their rooms. Remember the LLL Lemon Aid Law!

✻ Icons

You are exposed to icons every day, particularly if you use a computer. When you want to print a document, you know to click on the small drawing of a printer. If you want to save a document, you click on the drawing of the little floppy disk. Humans think in pictures, not words, so icons are very powerful.

If someone needs a massage or facial, what picture comes to mind? If you're a massage therapist, you want an image that represents your business to be the first thing they think of. If your product is jewelry, what icon or picture can you develop and use that connotes jewelry?

> What item will identify your company so people will remember you?

Many business owners and sales representatives use their names, and rightly so, to identify themselves. My suggestion, however, is to do the *TWIST* and identify yourself and your business with an object; if your name is an object that can be related to your business, you're in luck! You can also create a logo, which can become your icon, much like the Nike swoosh mark.

Years ago when I was developing my marketing business, I knew I needed something easily memorable for clients and prospects to identify with. I've always loved to cook and have been fascinated with food, so that's where I began.

At the time, my husband and I had just sold a business that left us in a very sour situation. I remember commenting to him one day, "We can be bitter or we can

make things better." That phrase, which I repeated a lot during those days, reminded me of a lemon. Oh, I know a lot of people use the trite saying, "When life gives you lemons, make lemonade," but I wondered about people who don't like lemonade. What should they do with all the lemons in their lives? As I looked at recipes with lemon as an ingredient, it dawned on me that while a lemon is sour and sometimes is the star flavor for lemon meringue pie, lemon bars, and lemon pound cake, it can also be used in recipes for other purposes, depending on the *TWIST* it is given.

One thought led to another and I decided my desire was to teach people how to look at the sour situations in life and business with a different—even fresh—perspective, which I dubbed the *TWIST*. And because business owners, sales representatives and independent consultants have a business to build, it's a situation similar to the lemonade stands of youth, the object being to find customers and sell product.

As you decide on an identifying visual mark, use it in all your marketing and promotions, including the color schemes, and brand your website around it. A pictorial-based icon can be worth millions of customers!

✻ Internet

The Internet has been one of the best ways to find customers not only in groups outside of your family and friends but also outside of your city, state, and country! You would not be reading this book today if it weren't for the Internet because that's how I "accidentally" began my business as The Lemon Aid Lady.

My Internet Story: Back in 1998 when I wrote the first edition of this book, (which, by the way, had a total of two paragraphs about finding customers on line!), I printed two hundred copies and figured I'd find *thirsty* audiences to present to and then sell the book, which I did for the first two months. My audiences were small, fewer than 25 business owners. Then my phone started to ring with orders. At first I thought a couple of my customers might have told their friends about the book at sales meetings, but then I got smart and began asking people, "Who can I thank for referring you to our company" (a question I still ask new customers so I know where leads are coming from and also so I know who to thank for the referral). Over and over the response was, "an on line group."

At that time, I had an e-mail address and occasionally used the Internet for this, but had not even thought of having my own website. I knew, however, that I had to find out what these "groups" were. I discovered I could create my own free newsgroup to which I could send out messages and information. This was the beginning of my on line marketing. Every other week, I'd send an e-mail with a creative business-building idea which generated more phone calls for my book and, better yet, found more people joining my on line group. Soon, the two hundred books were sold and that edition was reprinted several times. This newsgroup was also the channel for people to sample my "sips" of information and then request me to present at their meetings. Before I knew it, my audiences were in the hundreds, then thousands of *thirsty* people who bought my books, joined my newsgroup, and told their friends about The Lemon Aid Lady.

Within a couple of years (I can't believe it took me that long!) one of my customers suggested I hire her husband to create a website for me so people could order on line. In those days, building a website with a shopping cart was expensive—as in thousands of dollars—but it was worth it because this was how people across the world met me.

Things certainly have progressed since early 2000. Now, an average person can create and upload a website within hours! With progression comes competition; one cannot expect business to come flocking to your site just because it is live. No, Internet marketing can literally be a worldwide tangled web! I have invested heavily in both time and money for information from some of the best Internet marketing experts in the world and suggest you do the same if you want more in-depth suggestions on specific on line tools. Here I teach the simple, virtually no-cost ways that I've used to find more customers with one of THE most effective ways to find customers, the Internet.

Website: Years ago, you might have been asked, "Do you have a website?" In today's market, people expect that you have a website and ask for your web address as naturally as they once asked for your telephone number.
Your websites (yes, you need more than one) should be designed to attract two kinds of people: Those you know and those you don't!

Those you know can find you easily if your domain name is simple to remember. As The Lemon Aid Lady, my domain name is www.LemonAidLady.com. You'll notice this is not spelled like the drink lemonade, so I also purchased the domain name

www.LemonadeLady.com and pointed it to my site. If you know me as The Lemon Aid Lady, you'll probably figure out how to find me. If you do a search for Lemon Aid Lady, I'll pop up on the first page. Which is great, *if you know me.*

What about those who don't know me (or you) yet? This is where Internet marketing really kicks in and you'll need to design your sites around the terms that are most often searched when people are *thirsty* for your product, they are called key words. You might be reading this book after visiting my site specific to the topic of finding customers at www.WhereToFindCustomers.com.

Or you might have purchased one of my inspirational cookbooks at www.CookINspiration.com.

This is the aspect of Internet marketing that takes time and practice; we work on it every day in our business to attract *thirsty* people to visit our sites, and you'll have to do it as well. The best on line tools I've used for this purpose are newsletters, blogs, social networking, articles, and videos. Additionally, I do the *TWIST:* I research using these same tools to go out and invite prospects to do business with me. Here are some tips to bring people to your site as well as *TWISTS* to go out and find customers for each tool:

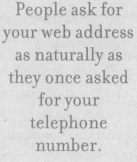

People ask for your web address as naturally as they once asked for your telephone number.

Electronic Newsletters: This is my favorite way to meet and keep customers because it's how I first created an Internet presence, and it's still the main tool I use to attract prospects with business-building information. My subscribers in turn refer me to their associates. My newsgroup from long ago, which was free but included advertisements from other companies, is now provided through my shopping cart service, so it's extremely affordable.

Each of my websites has a newsletter; the distribution schedule of each depends on my purpose and audience; some are weekly, others bi-monthly or monthly. Frequency is not as important as consistency. I schedule my newsletters just like I schedule face-to-face meetings with important clients and prospects, meaning I show up regularly! Be sure that every page of your website has a place for people to sign up as prospects don't always go to your home page first, or sometimes ever.

If your website is managed by a parent company or corporation and you're not able to customize it with sign up boxes, you can add to your subscriber list when you meet people in person, at events, when they order, or with a request in your e-mail signature line instructing *thirsty* people to send you an e-mail so you can add them to your distribution list.

> Schedule newsletters just like face-to-face meetings with important clients and prospects; show up regularly.

When prospects subscribe to the newsletter, take them to a page with a one-time offer—this is their only chance to get the product or the product with that special deal. Additionally, you can send them a gift certificate for a future purchase when they take advantage of this initial offer. Now you have a subscriber, and a customer, too!

I subscribe to a lot of on line newsletters, as most of you and your customers might, so I keep mine easy to read so they'll be opened. In the past, I used services with a lot of flash, flair and fashion and got okay results. Then I learned that newsletters which are text-based, rather than all the colors and options (html), have a greater open rate. So, here's what I do now:

Each newsletter includes an awesome article, *sprinkled throughout with keywords* appropriate to my website. But instead of putting the article in the body of the newsletter, I add a link to the article on my website which is more attractive and colorful than the text e-mail. In order to get people to click on the article, I have an attention-getting sentence or two and instruct:

Click here to discover how to (Place the link)

When using text only, you can use other characters to highlight the link such as:

Click here to discover how <<<< <<<<<< (Place the link)

When they get to the article, subscribers are thrilled to have these great ideas. I also have an image of a product on the side margin of the page; it's a subtle advertisement that doesn't get in the way of the information.

Keep the articles short so people can read and forward them quickly. I like to write a series of articles on the same subject so each week my subscribers anticipate the information. At the end of each article I write a teaser for the next issue and remind them to forward the article in its entirety to their friends.

At the bottom of the article, I have a link to that issue's featured product or weekly offer with a few lines of ad copy and an explanation. I've had a handful of people in the past say they don't like my advertisements, but I can't listen to their whining: all the free information on and off line is supported through advertisements.

Divide the newsletter "segments" with separator characters from the keyboard:

++++++++++++++ Plus sign
//////////////////// Slash, same key as question mark character
*********** Asterisk made from upper case of numeral 8
^^^^^^^^^^^ Arrow made from upper case of number 6
<><><><><><> Design made from alternating forward and backward
           arrows.

Create your own text dividers so people can easily read the segments.

Featured Product: The next segment of the newsletter is a blurb about a new product, featured product, or upcoming event. It's only a few sentences with, once again, a link to a full page of information contained on the website. Yes, this link is the same link I have at the bottom of the article page. This way, if they read the article but don't come back to the newsletter, they are still going where I want them to go.

> Take new
> subscribers to a
> page with a
> one-time only,
> great offer!

Winners: The third and last (I told you it would be short and sweet) is a segment where I honor a subscriber (once again, divided with some of the characters previously shown) and award him or her with a product.

I pull information off their profile and mask it so I don't divulge any private details. I list three or four "clues" and if they meet all of them, they are the winner and must call me by a designated time (I usually give about 48 hours), and they'll get the product free.

Some of the data I list as clues:

✳ First or last name (Don't list both for privacy)
✳ Initials
✳ Name of company
✳ E-mail provider
✳ First few letters/numbers of e-mail
✳ Date they signed up as a subscriber
✳ Zip code (on file only if they've purchased)
✳ Last 4 digits of phone number (on file only if they've purchased)

These clues are much more fun than just announcing their name. From time to time, I have people who mistakenly call, forgetting every clue must pertain to them. In that case, I usually send them a token souvenir for being bold and making the call.

I put "Winners" at the bottom of the newsletter because I want recipients to read the entire newsletter. Since I advertise that I choose winners in each issue when they register, most of them will scroll down and read the entire few paragraphs which comprise my newsletter.

> Include your phone number in your newsletter as well as an opt-out option.

Signature Line: Even though most people will communicate via e-mail, I always list my office number under my name in case someone prefers calling me.

Newsletter Summary: You can choose any segments to put in your newsletter, just remember to keep it easy to read and respond to. Never harvest names or spam anyone. And, always invite your subscribers to encourage their friends to subscribe. Be sure you have an "opt out" feature so people can automatically unsubscribe at any time. To read samples of my newsletters, sign up at one of my websites listed above.

Now, a TWIST on newsletters: Search on line for newsletters that are both complimentary to and competitive with yours and become a subscriber. I have a separate e-mail set up just for this purpose. You'll be able to see what other topics your *thirsty* prospects have available to them and you might want to trade (don't copy or steal) articles with the author or place an ad in their newsletter. If the newsletter addresses the same *thirsty* people but has different topics from your expertise, perhaps you could do some joint ventures with the website

owner. For example, I teach sales, marketing, and leadership to business own-ers; my friend and CPA Vicky Collins teaches the same audiences about taxes. Our services complement one another and we've been able to introduce each other to our own customers.

Blogs: This was one Internet tool that I resisted because I thought it would invade my privacy. The idea of a web log (thus the term blog) led me to believe I had to write a daily diary for anyone to read. I suppose you could do this in your personal life, but for your business, blogging is simply adding posts, or ideas, for your cus-tomers to read. If you want customers, not just readers, be sure to add your prod-ucts to the blog and links to your website.

You can use free blogs, and I have before, but that format is not business profes-sional. Free blog software is available where you can use your own domain names and your own web host.

Blog TWISTS: Search for blogs written by *thirsty* people. For instance, if your prod-uct is related to clothing, makeup, or hairstyle, search for blogs written by people who need to have a sharp, professional image, such as professional presenters. Do an on line search to find these blogs so you can read the posts and add com-ments. When you comment, some blogs show your website so *thirsty* readers can be linked to you. Use etiquette here and don't post a comment to promote your-self. First of all, the comment will probably not be accepted if posts have to be approved. I report these kinds of posts as spam when reviewing comments on my blog. Secondly, you look like a pushy self-promoter and no one will want to click on your link anyway!

Social Networking: Like many folks, my favorite social network site is Facebook. Currently, there are three ways to use Facebook: Personal profiles, Groups, and Pages.

Personal pages: I love connecting with people I haven't heard from in years. It's like getting an annual holiday letter every time an "old" friend invites me to be a friend or I find someone I haven't heard from for years. Whenever I read about what my friends across the world are doing, I feel connected, which is the best way to strengthen relationships and find customers. One night I was in a hotel writing this book and I posted this status update on my personal profile:

"Cruisin' through central Illinois (have never seen so many corn fields!) going to the Corvette FunFest in Effingham. Well...Bob's going to show off his awesome car while I stay at the hotel to finish my new book."

One of my Facebook friends (someone I've known since grade school but would never have connected with had it not been for social networking) posted:

"A new book you're reading or writing?"

I sent a reply with a link to pre-order the book and then other friends joined the conversation with comments like:

"I didn't realize you were a famous author. I am so proud to say I knew you when. You always did give the best demos."

When I updated my status I wasn't looking to promote the book at all, yet now my personal friends from long ago *and their friends* have been introduced to this book.

> Read status updates of friends who announce their sour situations and comment with a suggestion using your expertise and product.

TWIST: On my personal profile, I lurk more than post. I love to read status updates of friends who announce their sour situations. Then I can send a comment and suggest an idea. One of my friends once commented about how sick her kids had been and that she'd bleached her entire house to kill germs. One of her friends commented that bleach isn't very safe. I added a comment suggesting my friend check out one of my client's products as a safe, green alternative. Once again, my friend—along with her "friends"—now know about my client's product.

You can create groups on Facebook and invite your friends, which, like the personal profile, is limited to 5,000 friends. To spread the word about your business and find *unlimited thirsty* customers, who are known as "Facebook Fans," you'll want to set up business pages. Yes, you can have more than one page.

To set up a page (this process can be updated by Facebook at any time):

* Scroll to the bottom of your Facebook page
* Click on Advertising (it's in a tiny typeface)
* The page that appears says "Facebook Advertising"
* Look at the top left side for the yellow flag icon (under the blue bar with your name); click on word "Pages" to the right of the Fan Flag
* This page is called "Facebook Pages" and contains some great information
* Continue the set up process by clicking on the Green rectangle to the far right
* "Create New Facebook Page" appears. Choose which category you want to be listed under and name your page. For best results, choose words that *thirsty* prospects would use in a search
* Click the blue rectangle that says "Create a Page"
* Now your page is set up and you can choose the options you want from there

Articles: When you write keyword-focused articles to post on your website or to include in your newsletter, submit them to sites which have libraries of articles on thousands of topics. When people visit these sites and type in key words that match your article, you've found a *thirsty* prospect! Be sure to follow the guidelines for each site so your articles are accepted and read. The one I use most often is ezinearticles.com.

TWIST: Once again, go out and search for people who market to the same *thirsty* people as you do as well as read articles written by people who could be *thirsty* for your product or service.

Videos: You can upload videos to your site or to video sites, especially those specific to your *thirsty* prospects. Short, on line videos can introduce the world to you and your product...fast. Prospects can meet you on demand. YouTube is the most popular, and when you upload videos there, be sure to add the key words your *thirsty* prospects will be typing in. Always include your website and other contact information.

TWISTS: Do a search for the *thirsty* people you're trying to meet. If you sell pet supplies, watch for people who post videos with animals. Imagine...getting paid for watching videos! It's possible when you do the *TWIST.*

Blend the Internet with Other Marketing Tools: Internet marketing, in my experience, is enhanced when combined with other modes of communication. For example, you might have this information today because you received a postcard from me inviting you to visit www.WhereToFindCustomers.com and attend a free TelAdventure. Or maybe you met me at a home show and purchased one of my inspirational cookbooks which enticed you to visit my on line store.

Direct mail, personal phone calls, or face-to-face invitations can increase your website traffic, especially when you take prospects on a website tour. Read more about this concept in the W section of this book.

✳ Jewel Mail

Why do people complain about junk mail? Because it's unsolicited and thrown out with the junk. Change your *TWIST* on this and a whole new world opens up. You'll now look at this type of mail as **jewel mail.**

Why is it jewel mail? Because the mail becomes valuable to you in the following ways:

1. See how other people are marketing their products. Are they using creative mail pieces or conducting promotions that could be adapted to your business?
2. What do the pieces say? Collect those that just "grab" you. Maybe a headline could be adapted to your product. I am not suggesting to steal ideas, but to adapt them (although savvy marketers keep these samples in what is called a swipe file—ideas that are swiped from others). And when you do a *TWIST* as you examine this newly discovered jewel mail, you'll come up with new ideas of your own.
3. Local business that you could do cross-promotions and barter with.
4. Is this a medium that you'd like to advertise in? Call other businesses and see if they like it.
5. Keep this organized in a file according to how you'll use the pieces.
6. And, if you like what the advertiser has to offer, patronize them.

> Jewel mail can add value and sparkle to your business.

✳ Jump Start

Have you ever left your car lights on and drained the battery? What do you do? Ask someone to give you a "jump!" I know I've had a lot of requests for this and my good husband is always willing to assist a traveler in need.

If your company has been drained of new customers and profits, maybe you need a jump start. And where do you turn? To someone who has more stored energy than you do! This is the time to ask for the aid of a sales leader or mentor; not to do the work for you but to go to work with you.

While I was in the waiting room at a doctor's office one day, I saw two professionally dressed men walk in together. As they signed in with the receptionist, I realized they were pharmaceutical representatives, so I began a conversation with them. I assumed one was new and the other was the expert. However, they were both seasoned professionals, but they were working together to "jump start" the accounts in my city.

When you run out of customers, don't run away; race to the person who has stored expertise, energy, and enthusiasm and soon you'll have more customers running to you!

✳ Key Chains

Purchase unique key chains when you are in cities other than your own. While working in Orlando, I found some customized key chains printed with names and decorated with Disney characters that were marked down and put in the bargain bin. My guess is that while the names were not strange, they were not as common as Mary and Sally. I put these key chains on my own ring of keys. When I'd be standing in line or at any of the hundreds of potential business situations I found myself in, my key chain would be a real attention-getter! I'd ask people, "Do you know anyone with the name of Ashlee?" It was amazing that someone always knew someone with the names on my key chains, even though the spelling might have been different. While I was looking for people with these names so I could award them with the gift, I met others who were *thirsty* to hear about my business.

Be on the lookout for unique, personalized key chains. A good time to buy these is when you find a close out sale. Usually the ones that haven't sold are those with really unique names; these are the new customers you'll be looking for. Put the key chains on your own personal key ring. This will make your keys heavy, so every time you use your keys, you'll be reminded that you need to find these people. When you're standing in line, at a demonstration, event, or in any other situation when you're carrying your keys (be sure they are visible), people will ask you about them. Then you can explain that you are looking for people with these names so that you can service their needs with your product/service.

Once you give out a key chain, replenish it with another one so you are constantly using this system and gaining new customers.

When you do find people with these names, introduce yourself and your business to them. Even if they don't begin a business relationship with you right away, give them the key chain. They won't forget you. And remember that "No" never means never. You now have the potential for future business.

> "No" never means never!

If you don't meet people with these names face-to-face, ask the people you do meet if they know folks with these names. In fact, the best thing is when you have to really hunt for these special people because, in the meantime, you are meeting many other potential customers.

If your company provides a car as a bonus, or if you're a car or home salesperson (products that need keys to be opened) you'll want to try this suggestion right away—tell the prospect this is the key chain to the future!

✳ Kids

Kids are not only a prime marketing group for products and services they "must have," they can also help you promote your business. Give free t-shirts to customers' children, create advertising souvenirs that kids will be excited to use, and host coloring contests with kid-themed prizes even if your product is not targeted to kids. When you need inexpensive labor to deliver flyers or catalogs, invite pre-teens to do it.

If you have children of your own, they can be a great advertisement by wearing logo clothes and using your products. And, because they live with you and see you working your business, they can easily tell others (teachers and friends' parents) about it.

I ran a home-based, direct sales business while my sons were growing up. Even though they might not have admitted it, they were great advertisements as they told their friends about the company cars, vacations, and prizes I qualified for (especially when I volunteered to drive for car pools, sports teams and school functions).

If you have a retail establishment, carve out a "Kid Corner" if you have space that's conducive to having children in the building. The kids might actually request to come to your store so they can play! We owned a business where we serviced hundreds of direct-selling moms, so we placed a play tent in the building to keep the kids occupied while their mothers were picking up their orders. While one group of moms was conducting business, the moms in line watched the kids; it worked out very well.

> When you show how your product benefits families, kids will encourage their parents to buy.

Host events or presentations for moms and daughters, moms and sons, dads and sons, and the most popular—Daddy Daughter Dates. When you show how your product benefits families, kids will encourage their parents to buy. Because children are so honest, they make great sales "representatives;" unlike adults, they are not afraid to open their mouths!

✳ Kiosks

These mini-retail establishments, which are a cross between a retail establishment and a vendor event (expos/art fairs, craft shows) have gained a lot of popularity over the past few years. Renting or leasing a kiosk in a busy mall (the key word is "busy") could be a great place to find *thirsty* customers. Kiosks become natural "hang outs" if you have a hook to get people to stop by. While you're not paying for a lot of square footage, the fees can be high, depending on the season. Also, you typically have to be open during all hours of the mall, so this is best used when you have employees or other consultants to work with.

In the past few years several direct sales companies I've worked with have opened kiosks during holiday times. Consultants tell me that the exposure of mall shoppers to their company is worth the time and dollar investment because they meet large numbers of people who become future customers and host home parties that take them through a year and more of sales. Once again, the focus is not always on the sales you make, but the leads you meet, so be positive to gather the contact information of each guest to your kiosk even if a purchase is not made.

✳ Laundry Mat

Doing laundry probably isn't anyone's favorite activity, but when laundry can't be done at home, this chore is even worse! Even if you don't have laundry to do, you can visit laundry mats to find customers. Remember that you have a captive audience because people have to sit and wait for the machines to do the work. Give them something to do, like shop in your catalog or read flyers you've posted.

If you have to use the laundry mat for your own clothes, use your time wisely and begin conversations with other folks who are waiting for their wash. If you have work to do, such as assembling advertising packets or adding labels to your products or literature, do this while you're waiting for your clothes; other customers might approach you to ask about your company.

For network marketing reps, this is a great place for recruiting because you have an opportunity where people can earn money to buy their own washer and dryer. Maybe they live in an apartment and don't have room or outlets for washers and dryers. Your company could be the vehicle they need to save money for a house! Sometimes people do laundry at a laundry mat because their washer is broken. Once again, you can introduce them to a money-making venture.

✳ Library

One way to grow your business is to expand your mind. I recommend monthly trips to your local library. How does this bring new leads to you? Check out books that

are related to your product/service, because as you learn from them you become an expert people will trust. And as you read, you know not to mark your place in the book by turning the pages down, right? So, what should you use for a bookmark? Your business card works really well, or any small piece of literature, like a brochure.

When you return the book, leave your bookmark in the book for the next person, because when they check out the book, not only do they have a bookmark, but you have a potentially *thirsty* audience for your product! If you sell kitchen items, check out cookbooks for new ideas and leave your "bookmark" in the book. When people think of the book's subject, they'll relate it to you and want to give you a call! If you own an appliance repair business, read about appliances and donate your business card as a bookmark. If someone has checked out this book because they need to fix their dishwasher, they might give you a call instead.

> Not only does the next reader have a built-in bookmark, but you have a potentially *thirsty* audience for your product!

No fair "bookmark dumping" (placing your cards in every book on the shelf) as this turns your literature into litter!

Newspapers from other communities around the country are often at local libraries and offer you an excellent source for leads. Yes, you can read some of these papers on line, but not every page of every paper is posted electronically.

Story Time is where you can meet parents if you have a family-related product.

Events held at libraries could give you an opportunity to display your business.

Lecture series are not only great to attend to meet others, but also to present your knowledge of your industry.

Bulletin Boards list what's going on in your community from fund raisers to lectures. Would attending and supporting these functions allow you to meet *thirsty* prospects?

✳ Lines

Whenever you're standing in line, especially when you're hanging out where *thirsty* leads might hang out, you have another captive audience to meet and get to know. People usually become bored while they are waiting, and if something doesn't interest or entertain them, they become agitated and even upset because of the wait! Open up a conversation with a compliment (see Lemon Aid Laws) and meet a new customer while waiting in line.

✳ Lists

When you want to remember something, you write it down. That's why we create "to do" and grocery lists. If you want to remember to find customers, write down a list of...

   ✳ *Where* you plan to find customers
   ✳ *How* you plan to find customers
   ✳ *Who* you plan to find as customers

Make your "where" and "how" lists from the ideas in this book. The "who" list can be as specific as someone you personally know (write the name down) or as broad as a group of *thirsty* people you want to connect with, such as Mothers of Multiple groups, high school teachers, persons who own watercraft and so on.

List only three-to-five (super-achievers, no more than ten!) at a time so you'll feel the success of accomplishment and not the agony of defeat.

✳ Literature

Literature is any written piece about you or your business that you distribute so prospects will remember you and have a reference for future communication. This includes flyers, business cards, post cards, catalogs, and company brochures. The more unique the literature, the more valuable it is, and the more people will keep

it. You can refer to the segments in this book for ideas on using, giving, and gathering these items.

Your literature leaves an impression of you; it's your "personal packaging," so be sure it's professional, clean, neat; always includes your name, website, and other contact information.

> The more unique the literature, the more valuable it is, and the more people will keep it.

✳ Logo Wear

This can be one of the easiest ways to attract prospects to your business while being fashionable at the same time! Today's consumers are accustomed to seeing names of companies on clothing. In fact, they often pay more money to wear a designer's name! This mindset makes people aware of what is printed on clothing. You'll be a walking billboard, and so will your employees, family and customers as you provide logo wear for sale (another way to add a few bucks to the business) or as give away incentives.

Logos are also great on non-clothing items such as duffel bags, golf bags, cosmetic cases, water bottles and such.

❋ Magazines

You'll be amazed as you walk down the aisles of magazines at local bookstores and check out the racks that are jam-packed with publications you've probably never heard of. The good news is that you're likely to find a handful that will be targeted to your *thirsty* prospects. Here are some ideas for finding customers while you read and research magazines. Most of these features are universal to all magazines.

Letters to the Editor: People who write to the editor generally do so to agree or disagree with a column or feature in a previous issue, and will often back their opinion with a personal experience. In such cases, they divulge either a sour situation or sweet solution. Could you have the answer this person is looking for? Or, could you write a complimentary or congratulatory letter? How do you get in touch with these possible prospects? Some writers have an e-mail address which makes corresponding very easy; most have a city and state listed so you can look them up on line if their contact information is public.

Tips to Share: This is where readers submit their ideas related to interests of the magazine audience. Use the ideas you read and send thank you notes to the contributors; add product literature, business cards or gift certificates for your product as a token of appreciation.

As you read the tips, do the *TWIST* and ask if yourself if your product would enhance, compliment, or eliminate the need for the tip. I cannot tell you how many times I've seen a tip in a cooking magazine that suggested adding a slice of apple

134

or bread to the brown sugar so it doesn't get hard as a rock! Yet, if the sugar is stored in an airtight container (such as Tupperware) the brown sugar wouldn't get hard in the first place!

If available and appropriate, send a sample to the contributor along with information about your company.

How-to articles: Every magazine is full of "how-to" features. Read the article thoroughly, and learn from it. Then ask yourself, "What information could I share with the author that would add to his?" Do you have a product that would solve one of the problems presented in the article? If you have a business opportunity to offer, it might be of interest to the author.

An author who wrote about dealing with a family's food budget might be very interested in your coupon redemption business. You could contact the person who wrote "How to Stay Out of Court" if you sell a pre-paid legal service.

> Would your product enhance, compliment, or eliminate the need for the tip?

You can contact the magazine for the address, e-mail or phone number of the author (most work on a freelance basis). My husband is a journalist, and magazines forward responses from readers to him very often. Do keep in mind that not all authors will be open to your ideas, but you'll never know until you try. If they are not interested, ask them for referrals. Because they are an expert in their field, they might have a gold mine of referrals or mention your business in an upcoming article. If a magazine accepts unsolicited articles, write and submit one. You could be the next featured expert.

Special Interest Stories: These stories highlight a person or group who has done something of special interest. This person might have begun a community project, volunteered for or donated to a worthy cause, or overcome a great obstacle. In this case, you want to contact the person the story is about, not the author. Compliment them on their accomplishment. Show them how you can promote their cause. Can you offer a fund raiser for their organization? Can you donate something to their mission? You don't always have to sell them something. In fact, for stories like this, where the featured person has given so much, your contribution would be appreciated, and when you give, you will eventually receive.

Recognition Stories: These stories are written to showcase someone's accomplishments. The story could be a multi-page cover feature or just a small blurb hidden among other text. You have to be a detective! Since the person is being highlighted because of an accomplishment, a complimentary or congratulatory note would be appropriate. Of course, include your business card and other literature.

"I'm looking for..." Some magazines have an open column for readers to ask the general readership for information. I've seen columns requesting recipes, computers, car parts, best places to eat, on and on... Perhaps your product/ service would fill the needs and wants of some of these people. Send them a reply (most of these columns give ways to contact the individual directly) along with your literature.

Contests: Magazines often run contests in conjunction with their advertisers. Enter the contests, and you might get to meet other contestants when you become a finalist! And if you don't make it that far, watch for when the winners are announced in the magazine so you can send each one a congratulatory note and an awesome offer for one of your products that will remind them of their great achievement.

> Enter contests, sign up for committees, and join communities of magazines targeted to your *thirsty* audience.

Committees and Communities: Magazine editors value feedback from readers so much they set up committees and communities so subscribers can be on special panels and focus groups. This way, they come to understand what "real" readers really want. Then these people—maybe you— are interviewed and featured in stories. What a great way to publicize your business!

Social Networking: Most magazines invite readers to follow them on Twitter or to be their fan on Facebook. Accept the invitations so you can read what these *thirsty* prospects are cheering or complaining about.

Send samples to the department editors of the magazines. This might be a long shot at getting some publicity, but you never know till you try! It could also be the start of a relationship with a magazine's subscribers.

✴ Magnets

To get *thirsty* people to "stick" with you, give them something that sticks to their refrigerator, file cabinets, washing machine, dryers, cars, or chalk boards. The best thing is your business card because your name and logo will be in their view when they use this equipment. And, when they have visitors to their home or office, they'll be your billboard to show off your company with your magnet.

Here's a great *TWIST:* While walking through parking lots, watch for cars that belong to *thirsty* prospects and leave a business card magnet on their car door. Let's say you offer a pet grooming service. As you walk through the parking lot, watch for cars with dogs inside, bumper stickers indicating they are pet owners, big bags of pet food sitting on the seat, or a leash hanging from the rear view mirror. Carefully place your magnet—you don't want to scratch any paint or set off alarms—near the handle of the driver's side; they'll be pleasantly surprised you left them a gift on the door.

When I walk through neighborhoods to meet new prospects, if the occupant is not home and the front door is steel, I leave a magnet. One time, the homeowner called me even before I arrived back to my house!

You can also have advertising souvenirs that adhere magnetically, such as bottle openers, picture frames, pens, and more.

✴ Mailing Pieces

Instead of mailing a one-page flyer, send offers and announcements in one envelope—preferably a colored one—with several pieces. It creates curiosity for the recipient. They thumb through the envelope and want to look at all the potential treasures rather than reading pages of text.

My experience has been to use 4" x 6" envelopes (preferably attractive, colored ones) and printed cards (colored cardstock or bond paper). The mailer is essentially one sheet cut up into several pieces, each having great information and offers: gift certificates or coupons with varying valid dates, testimonials, or something the

recipient will want to save (recipes, tip charts, or inspirational quotations). This makes opening the mail a lot more fun for your potential customers and profitable for you.

Direct sales and party plan people can use this concept when sending invitations to home parties; a real *TWIST* on the traditional post cards with investing only a few more cents per piece.

✳ Malls

When I'm at malls, I like to shop for customers as much as for bargains. You can, too!

But never stalk prospects and twist their arms to buy your product—this is absolutely contrary to my version of the *TWIST*. Rather, sit on benches in the common areas or observe people while you're window shopping; you'll be surprised at how much people really advertise what they need with their actions!

For example, you notice an older couple hobbling along holding hands, and they sit down next to you. Strike up a conversation about what's ailing them (they'll tell you!) and lead the conversation to tell them about your chiropractic services.

Take a field trip to the local mall and use the Lemon Aid Laws. You really will end up with bags of new prospects because you're watching, not stalking, for *thirsty* people.

✳ Neighborhoods

In my opinion, the automatic garage door opener is to blame for the reduction of neighborliness! When we leave our homes, we get into our cars through the comfort of our garages. We press a button to open the door, then we back the car out without acknowledging others who might be in their yard or walking down the street. As we leave the driveway, we press that button again to close the garage door—thus securing our house—and we're on our way! It's little wonder that many people search the Internet to meet new friends. We've become a nation where neighbors are strangers and strangers are neighbors.

As I consult with start-up companies that aren't limited by geographic sales territories, the sales leaders are always anxious to plan which cities they are going to conquer without looking in their own neighborhood first, where golden contacts could abound. While these ideas work well for home-based businesses, you can adapt them to any market by creating your own *TWIST*s. Use these ideas to build in your own backyard before you expand into other borders:

> We've become a nation where neighbors are strangers and strangers are neighbors.

Let everyone in your neighborhood knows what product/service you sell. As soon as you move to a new area or begin your new business, host a Grand Opening showcasing your products or services. This can be done in either your home or place of business. The purpose of this event is to get to know your neighbors. Invite them by personally visiting them at their homes to introduce yourself. If the person is not home, leave an invitation (but do not tape it to the door; that's tacky!).

When you have the opportunity to meet your neighbors in person, ask for their phone number or e-mail so you can personally remind them about the Grand Opening. I've heard many experiences where people have mailed and distributed hundreds of flyers for these events and only a couple of people show up. Remember: You work in a relationship business. People will do business with you when they know you, and are confident that you care about them.

To encourage business from your neighborhood—if it's appropriate for your industry or market— put a yard sign out that reads _____ (company name) sold here. You'll want to check for local ordinances concerning signs as well as the use of your company's name if you don't already have rights to use the name/logo.

> ### Host a "Neighbor Appreciation Day"

Once or twice a year, host a "Neighbor Appreciation Day" where you only invite the neighbors for specials on your products or services. Of course, encourage them to bring friends; but the personal invitation only goes right to the neighbors. Make them feel special because they are *your* neighbor!

Neighbors of your customers. Many of your customers don't know their neighbors, so if your business model is where you go out to meet with your clients or deliver products to their home, take a couple of extra minutes and drop by the homes of the people on both sides of your customer. I've used this approach when I've scheduled an appointment with a customer or prospect and they have forgotten and weren't home. I didn't want my trip to that neighborhood to be wasted, so I visited with the neighbors instead.

Go for a walk. One way to connect with neighbors is to go for walks. Recently, as my husband and I were beginning our walk, we met two new neighbors and had a lengthy visit. The conversation led to sharing with each other "what we do." A very casual, very simple way to find *thirsty* prospects.

When you go for a walk, you'll be able to observe more closely your neighbors and their surroundings. For example, you'll notice which houses are for sale, and which ones have sold and now have new occupants. Is your product something new homeowners are really *thirsty* for? Take a "Welcome to the Neighborhood" treat basket with edible goodies—along with your phone number, in case they have questions

about their new city or are in need of something. And what better way to give your phone number than your business card or product catalog?

Walking in the morning is a great time because you see which families have children getting on the school bus or are buckling babies in car seats, presumably to go to the day care center on the way to work. Once I observed that one neighbor had a daycare at her home because several cars pulled up and parents took children inside. Would this be a *thirsty* prospect for you?

> Pay attention to your neighborhood trash, and you could meet more customers and earn more cash!

The best mornings to walk are on trash pick-up day. Yes, you read that correctly. I love to see what kinds of boxes are being thrown out because I learn who has babies (they're throwing out boxes from a high chair or disposable diapers); I know who has purchased new computers and audio equipment (computer boxes); and I can tell who just purchased a treadmill (another box!).

✳ Networking

My husband, Bob, and I have had the opportunity of playing "matchmakers" for a few couples. Seeing people in happy relationships like ours brings us joy, knowing that we were the vehicle to their meeting. Matchmaking is really *networking*. Notice that our joy came because we connected people with each other; we didn't receive anything tangible from our efforts except a written invitation to a wedding!

You know people you do business with who might need the expertise of someone else you know. By networking, you "line" these individuals up. Now, you all benefit! Someday, the people you do business with will know someone who needs you and will be the vehicle for referring someone else to you. An excellent book to read on this subject is *Dig Your Well Before You're Thirsty* by Harvey Mackay. Actually, you should read all of his books for great business ideas!

Formal networking events are wonderful places for "matchmaking." Each group has different qualifications, methods, locations, and even fees. But the common denominator is that the purpose of the event is to broaden your net of people

looking for your *thirsty* prospects and theirs. Here are some suggestions for getting the most out of these meetings:

Be prepared with business cards, products, or advertising souvenirs.

Meet and mingle before and after the formal meeting begins.

Take notes as each attendee gives his brief presentation.

Stay within your time limit when you give your brief presentation; know exactly what you're going to say in the words that others could repeat so they remember what you do.

Describe a very specific kind of *thirsty* prospect you're looking for. If you want terrific leads you need to paint a vivid picture of the type of customer you're looking for so others at the meeting will begin to visualize your customer.

Let's go deeper into this discussion with an example. If you sell a fabulous line of linens, sheets, and towels and you want to market to people who own bed and breakfast inns, hit the bull's eye—a very targeted group of people—as you explain that your *thirsty* customer will:

❋ Own a bed and breakfast with at least four bedrooms
❋ Live in a town of at least 5,000
❋ Is open for business year round

Now the other meeting attendees know the profile of your *thirsty* customer and can be on the lookout for you.

Attend meetings regularly so you develop relationships with the other attendees.

> When other meeting attendees know the profile of your *thirsty* customer, they will be on the lookout for you.

Be patient. The expert networkers I know realize that in the beginning, they find more customers for others than the number of leads others bring them. That's okay, because after a while, you'll be flooded with referrals as people get to know who you are.

Change your customer profile. Continuing with the example above with the linen products...the next meeting your ideal customer might be someone who:

- ✳ Lives in a retirement community
- ✳ Is over sixty years old
- ✳ Hosts houseguests at least once a month

Visit other networking groups from time to time to be sure your net expands.

Yes, net working (I wrote the words separately so you can *see* that you've got to work your net) is all about spreading your net for prospects so it stretches outside of areas you probably wouldn't "fish" by yourself.

Remember that nets can bring in large catches, but they also have holes where the small, squirmy ones can fall out; they were not a *thirsty* catch for you!

✳ New People in the Area

People who are new to an area can feel lost and alone. Having moved across the country more times than I want to count, I know that people feel this way! A friendly "hello" and "welcome" from anyone is appreciated!

Look in the Club listings of your local community paper for any formally-organized clubs that cater to the needs of new people. The *Newcomers Club* is one such organization. I have done fund raisers for this organization before, and they go very well because the new people tend to be very cohesive. And, most join for at least a year. You can offer to do a presentation to the group for one of their monthly meetings to begin to establish a relationship with the club. The real key, however, is to meet the new people as they join. This way, you can personally welcome them to your area with a welcome basket. Ask the club officer for a listing of the new members.

> A welcome service should supply you with the contact information of all the new people who received a welcome gift.

Some areas have services that will send out mailings or deliver samples to new

residents. For a fee, you can include your information. If you choose this service, be absolutely *positive* that the supplier agrees to provide you with the names, phone numbers, e-mail addresses and home addresses of all the people that receive the mailing or samples so you can do your own follow through.

❋ Newspapers

Whenever we travel, I always buy the local papers so I get a feel for the community—and to get leads for my business! If you do want to expand across country without leaving your city, many papers provide on line versions at little or no fee.

Large metropolitan papers are very helpful; however, the smaller community papers seem to be a little more personal if you really want to get to know people. A combination of both works best!

Go through each section of the paper to determine whether *thirsty* prospects can be found in their readership. Here are a few suggestions:

> If you had no other source for leads, you could build a huge business just by dissecting the newspaper in the town or area you want to build.

Births: This section lists the new babies born along with the *parents names.* If families are your *thirsty* audience, you've found a real gold mine!!

Some of the very best sales consultants I ever recruited were found from new baby lists. This was a very *thirsty* audience for new moms who did not want to return to the workforce. Such was the case with Tina, whom I met after reading about the birth of her son. I called her on the phone and while she didn't agree to do business with me immediately, I faithfully called her back at the times she requested. Getting together with her took a while; in fact, it was after giving birth to her second child. She scheduled a home party and then *asked me* about joining my team. Eventually she promoted to a management position. Even though we don't work together any more, we keep in touch, and I consider her to be a great friend. This is a very fertile way to find new customers!

An important hint: file this section of the paper for a couple of weeks so that you're making these calls four to six weeks after the birth—if you call too soon, the parents will be really tired and might not be open to talking. During this waiting period, look up their phone numbers in the phone book or on line.

When I call, I generally make no reference to the fact that they have a new baby. I just want to know if they want my product. However, I have, at times, approached the call as a congratulatory one and offered to bring a gift by for the new mom. For me, that took more time than I could really spend. But, you might want to use that approach if you have an obvious product for the new baby market; you'll be welcomed with open arms. New moms might not want to discuss your business right then, so be prepared to call them back at a later time like I did for my friend Tina; it's worth the effort.

Community Calendar: Each paper seems to have a different name for this section; however, it is where meetings for clubs and organizations are listed. Which of these groups would be *thirsty* to know you and buy your product? You could offer to do a presentation to the group, help with a fund raiser, volunteer, or even join the organization if appropriate.

While reading this section, I discovered an association focused on families that would be a great match for a cross-promoting project with one of my consulting clients.

Business Section: *New hires and recent promotions* in the local business community are often listed, sometimes with a picture and brief business biography. Send a congratulatory note to the person and enclose your business card. At a later mailing or phone call, talk business more specifically. This is a wonderful way to network and to get referrals. If the person was transferred from another city or state, offer a welcome basket.

> Read more than just the stock listings when you check out the business section of your paper.

Grand Openings of New Businesses. Send the new business owners a "welcome and best wishes for success note." Do you see any possibilities for cross promoting and/or bartering?

Meeting and Seminar Announcements. As I read my paper's business section, I am amazed at the assortment of professional meetings. Expand your business by

attending meetings and seminars where you can learn and earn through networking with other professionals. Which group could use your product/service?

Awards and Recognitions. Business owners, especially those with small companies, love to be awarded and recognized. When you see stories of this nature, send a congratulatory note acknowledging their accomplishment. Enclose a business card. Do follow through contact for business development possibilities.

Achievements. Whenever you read about someone being recognized for personal, business, or scholastic achievements, a congratulatory note is in order. As I mentioned above, send a business card with your note. In the next contact—via phone, e-mail, mail, fax, etc.—offer them your service or product. Pay attention to children and teens; they are now part of a huge demographic buying group.

Fund Raisers: When a church, civic, school, or other group is hosting an event to raise money, the local newspaper usually carries an article. If the article lists a contact name, call that person to offer your type of fund raiser. Perhaps you'll want to attend the event to find out more about the organization. Support fund raisers as much as you can to get close to the decision makers so you can be considered for their next fund raiser.

Classified Advertising: Many small and home-based businesses with little or no advertising budgets list their services here in addition to consumers who want to sell items.

For example, someone seeking children for their day care would be a prime prospect if you sell anything related to child development, such as books, toys, software, and so on. If the advertiser lists her name, personalize the phone call by using it:

> "Hi, Jane, this is _____(your name) from _____(your company). I saw an ad in the paper about your day care service (this will get her attention!). Since you work with children, I have products that will _____ (list the benefits for her)."

From here, you would want to arrange to mail her information and/or samples or make an appointment to take her on a personal tour of your website. If time,

distance and circumstances permit, she might agree to a face-to-face meeting to see a demonstration of your product.

In another example, if someone is advertising a home for sale, they might need your carpet cleaning business. If a handyman lists that he paints homes and installs dry wall, he might be *thirsty* for the awesome, extreme dry hands lotion that you make and market.

For some joint business marketing, read the classifieds with a *TWIST* to determine which businesses or services are complimentary to your own. Let's again look at the example of homes for sale, which lists the name of the real estate agent. You could call the agent and suggest a cross promotion whereby you refer your carpet cleaning clients looking to sell their homes to him and he suggests you as the carpet cleaner when his clients list their homes. Share written literature and then offer specials for customers who work with both you and your cross-promoting partners.

> For some joint business marketing, read the classifieds with a *TWIST* to determine which businesses or services are complimentary to your own.

If you choose to advertise through this medium, I recommend that you do it regularly so people who read these ads will remember seeing you even if they don't need your service so when they do, they'll know exactly where to find you.

Garage Sales: For more details, turn to the G segment of this book.

Houses for Sale by Owner: This is the section that all real estate agents read first, hoping to convert this property to their own listing; this is effective. If you're not a real estate agent, what does someone who is moving need? Do you market lawn care or house cleaning services? Do you sell furniture or home decor? If nothing else, you'll know which homes are for sale, so when you know a home has sold, you have a new homeowner to meet who will want to know about the product or service you offer.

Society Page:
Wedding and Engagements. New brides and their husbands are often *thirsty* for products for their new home, so many companies market to them from the time a

couple is engaged up to their first few months of marriage. Smart marketers find the names of couples in the pages of local newspapers and do my *TWIST*: save the paper and then contact the newlyweds six to nine months *after* their big day. By this time, they're usually settled in their new home and now that the stream of gifts has trickled to a halt, they are ready to shop themselves.

Is your *thirsty* audience newly engaged couples? Do you offer a bridal registry or coordinate bridal showers? Here are names to call! The society page is usually where you can find the information. One store in my area even lists the couples who have registered on their bridal registry. Look these names up in the phone book.

Anniversaries and Birthdays. Send the couple celebrating their anniversary a card; do the same for the birthdays. Enclose your business card and a gift certificate for your product. I've seen some papers with baby pictures of one-year olds. Send the baby a birthday card and an offer for the parents.

> Contact newlyweds six to nine months after they say "I do."

Reunion listings. These are mostly in the community papers. See which group is having a reunion. Do you have a way to help them during their festivities? Maybe your band could be the entertainment. If they are doing an auction or drawings, offer them your product as a free or discounted gift; just be sure you get the name and phone number of the winner. If you cater dinners, this is a very *thirsty* market. If the organizers have already hired persons for these positions, ask if you can keep in touch with them for their next event.

Obituaries. This is obviously a sensitive area. Just like the baby list, I would not call anyone right away. Read the obituaries carefully to see if any of your friends, customers, or their relatives are listed here. If so, send a sympathy card with a copy of the obituary.

For those I don't know, I read for information. I've seen many young widows and widowers. Maybe my product will benefit them in the future. They might be looking for a business opportunity to supplement the lost income of the deceased spouse or to get out and meet people.

If you sell life insurance, here's a key place to find prospects. I want to emphasize the need to be sensitive and give the survivors some healing time before you approach them.

Cross Promoting Opportunities: The newspaper is chock-full of advertisements, large ones and small. Many small businesses use this advertising medium. Read the ads carefully; can you offer the business some cross-promotion opportunities? Would your product or service fill a need? These advertisements also give you great ideas for your own direct marketing campaigns.

✳ Offices

Because people are spending more and more time at work, many offices now allow sales and service folks to visit the work place and present their wares. Is your product or service conducive to this type of marketing?

You might be able to have a display in a conference room by yourself or a company might approve a group of vendors to have a themed event, such as a health care fair. Or, you could meet prospective customers because of your connection with one of the employees who takes your samples and product catalogs to work and places them in the common areas.

> Office Marketing is a convenience for employees.

These events are usually held before or after work, or during lunch breaks. Therefore, you need to be able to adapt your message to this type of audience.

Employers who are open to this concept view "Office Marketing" as a convenience for their employees…as long as it doesn't interfere or clash with their job duties and performance.

✳ Organizations

Which organizations are you currently a member of? Who in this organization needs your product/service? Just as I mentioned letting everyone in your

150

neighborhood know about your business, let everyone in the organizations to which you are a member know who you are and what you have to offer them.

And, which organizations would be compatible with your product? For instance, if you sell vitamins and nutritional supplements, you should join an organization that is actively involved in health-related issues.

Keep in mind that all organizations are looking to raise funds; can you solve their need?

✳ Outside

Outside can refer to several ideas:

Go outside the walls of your office, building, home, or store to find more custom-ers who haven't found you yet. The hardest door to open is usually your own! This might take you out of your comfort zone, but as long as you stay in your area of expertise, you should be eager and will-ing to stretch.

Go outside of your need to build your business and make profits. Instead, go out and influence and inspire others with your outstanding service, and customers will be attracted to you.

> The hardest door to open is usually your own!

Go outside of the pages of this book and contact my company if you're *thirsty* for in-depth education or company presentations on the topics I've discussed. E-mail me at Ideas@LemonAidLady.com or call 217-453-6007.

❊ Parades

March right up and find new customers by entering your company in a parade. This is a wonderful venue, especially if you live in a small town where the entrance fee is low or even free.

You can create a full-size float, enter your car, ride your decorated bike, or simply walk the parade route. Whichever way you choose, what parade watchers enjoy (especially kids) is receiving the candy and/or trinkets tossed by parade participants. If you throw these out to kids, attach them to business cards or other promotional literature. Include dated offers that will entice people to take action and call or go on line to purchase your products.

> Honor a group of customers by choosing them to ride on your company's parade float.

You don't have to do this alone, either. If you have a staff, involve them in the creation and decoration as well as being part of the parade as a person on a float, in a car, bike or a walk along. If you have other sales representatives in your area, invite them to join you. You can also include your customers and their families. This group will not only be honored, they'll also take a lot of photos with your company permanently placed in their albums, and will tell their family and friends to attend and watch.

After the parade, many communities have the floats parked in a nearby location, such as a park, where parade participants can visit with customers and prospects.

In some cases, vendor booths are part of the day's festivities and can be a good compliment to being in a parade.

✳ Parking Lots

Parking lots are valuable real estate, either at your own place of business or someone else's.

Your own: You can bring your business outside and host fun customer appreciation events where you hire entertainment and provide food and perhaps invite other complimentary vendors.

If you're overstocked on inventory, have a parking lot sale and display products under cabanas, or purposely plan annual parking lot sales events where you offer wonderful values.

Allow non-profit organizations to use your parking lot for their events such as garage sales or car washes. This is good exposure for your company.

Parking lots that belong to others: Look for a business that compliments your own and see if you can set up a display or mini kiosk. Grocery stores in my area allow outside food vendors to grill food for sale or youth groups to sell cookies or candy.

When I was a sales manager for Tupperware, a large, independently owned produce market opened near my home. Because people buying fresh food need storage containers, this was a perfect match. I met with the owner to ask permission and he was very open to the idea; he only asked that I not hand out a lot of literature that might end up littering the store. Once or twice a week my team and I would set up a small display in the back of one of our company vans. As customers walked through the parking lot we'd visit with them; we found a lot of very *thirsty* people. And before we left, we'd walk through the aisles of the store to pick up any of our catalogs or business cards left on the floor.

> Allow non-profit organizations to use your parking lot for their events such as garage sales or car washes.

❋ Parties

Social events like parties are opportunities to meet and visit people in settings where you really get to know them on a more personal level. Is it any wonder most conventions, trade shows, and educational events include some sort of social time apart from business activities?

> Meet new friends at casual parties and you'll have more prospect possibilities.

Parties do not have to be highly formal events in order to find customers; in fact, the more casual the party, the more opportunity you'll have to find prospects. It's especially fun when you attend a friend's party and don't know many of the other guests. You'll go home with new friends, and possibly potential prospects.

If, during the conversations, you realize someone you're talking to could be *thirsty* for your product or service, ask permission to contact them away from the party. Of course, you'll want to have a business card in your purse or pocket to hand them when they give you their contact information.

❋ Photos

Nearly everyone who owns a cell phone is carrying a camera! Coupled with the popularity of small digital cameras, taking pictures has become a regular occurrence in everyone's life.

Create a "Wall of Fame" in your business or office spotlighting your customers using your products. Attach testimonials as well. Or, place these photos in an album if you do sales demonstrations or presentations so prospects can see the types of customers you work with and the results they enjoy from using your products.

This is especially effective if your work enhances a prospect's physical appearance or environment such as make-up makeovers, weight loss products, orthodontic or dental procedures, plastic surgery, or home improvement projects (remodeling, or building).

✳ Post Cards

Mailing post cards as a marketing piece is effective because nothing has to be opened; prospects can see everything you want them to read as soon as the card is in their hand. Consequently, they stand out from the regular mail that people receive (most companies don't send their bills on post cards!). Cards this size can be mailed with a post card rate stamp, which reduces mailing costs.

A 4" x 6" post card also makes a great business card because people tend to keep it, not only because of its unique size but there is also room to print useful comments in addition to your contact information. If you hand this type of card directly to prospects, use the address area to pen a personal note, like a compliment.

> Use these colorful, fun pieces of "stationery" to thank, compliment, or appreciate an employee, customer or prospect.

This tool can be used for more than promoting you or your product. Use these colorful, fun pieces of "stationery" to thank, compliment, or appreciate an employee, customer or prospect. Anytime you can brighten someone's day, they will always remember you and your thoughtfulness. This is like the golden rule: treat others the way you'd like to be treated and everything will come back to you!

Post cards can be kept in a purse or brief case for taking quick notes so they can be written, and given or mailed easily.

✳ Post Office

As a business professional, you'll be making frequent visits to the post office. Be very observant while waiting in line. I look at what kinds of mail people are sending. If they have a lot of packages, ask if they have their own business. Many times the answer is yes, and I get to network with this person.

If your product or service has anything to do with stationery, paper goods, packaging, or communication you might find *thirsty* people at this venue.

Get to know the postal employees. Let them know what kind of business you have, and tell them about your successes. Invite them to do business with you and to tell others about your business. After all, they talk to people all day; your business should be stamped in their minds.

✳ Pregnant Women

These ladies are usually easy to notice, and soon-to-be-moms are a group with huge buying power. Cater to them before the birth of their new baby by designating parking spaces, chairs, and check out lanes just for them.

> The attention expectant moms receive from you before they deliver could influence the business they bring to your company for years after.

Create inexpensive pins that along with your company name and logo say, "My due date is _____" (they can write in the date with a permanent marker) to award all expectant moms who visit your business or place an order, even if your product has nothing to do with babies. The attention expectant moms receive from you before they deliver could influence the business they bring to your company for years after.

Offer a baby registry service if your products are used for a new baby or the needs of a new mom or her family. For example, if you own a fast food, grocery, or restaurant, create a gift certificate book for new moms redeemable for specific kinds of foods so meal planning will be taken care of for the first couple of weeks. This would make a great gift!

✳ Pre-Schools

Not to be confused with day care centers, pre-schools are specifically for children before they enter kindergarten. These could be run by nationally known chains, sponsored by churches, organized by community groups, or in many cases, schools that people run out of their homes.

If your product is educationally connected to children, parents, or families, contact the owners of these schools. Local newspapers and bulletin boards in grocery stores are the best place to find private individuals who run pre-schools. Also, ask parents of children who attend them for referrals.

Pre-schools usually have one or two fund raisers a year, so if you have a unique idea or product, this could be your *thirsty* audience. Perhaps your business would be a great field trip destination for the little "students". Encourage parents to accompany their children so they become familiar with your business.

✳ Product Attraction

Whether in your home, office, school, or other public place, you should wear, display, or use your product in any way you can.

People will approach you and ask where you found such a great item. Don't be shy and don't be salesy! Open your mouth and say, "This is part of my company's line" or "Glad you like it; it's one of my most popular pieces." And then add, "If you'd like one of your own, I'm your connection!" This response is so much better than, "I sell these great things." People hesitate talking to salespeople even in casual conversations. Keep the conversation focused on them and how you can be of service. Next to you, your product and product knowledge are your greatest advertisements.

> Find new customers by using your product!

✳ Presentations

Powerful presentations you give to individuals, clubs, committees, purchasing agents, or guests at home parties can lead you to more customers. As the saying goes, you only have one chance to make a first impression, so be prepared to make it with your product and knowledge.

Before the presentation, do your homework about the audience so you'll know how to present and position your product to their individual or group needs. Then add your own unique *TWISTs*. So many people use what I call electronic chalkboards

(Power Point) that an audience can become easily bored and distracted. Put your own personality in your show and think of alternatives to the computer (unless you're demonstrating a computer or software). I love using fun props that can engage the entire audience. It's best if your props are your products—when people experience your product you have less to explain.

> It's best if your props are your products – when people experience your product you have less to explain.

Be prepared to fill orders immediately by taking some inventory or by having order forms, pens, and other supplies handy. When people have "to think" about it, they often forget and forsake your offer. Understandably, some purchases could require more research and contemplation; you don't want to pressure them. Rather, be sure to gather the contact information of everyone at the presentation with a business card or door prize drawing forms so you can do follow up contacting.

❊ Promotions

If you want to promote purchases you must always have a promotion going on. My consulting company has been actively involved with our new city, Nauvoo, Illinois, to promote tourism. The town, like many communities, has three or four annual events each year which bring throngs of visitors to town. However, there are still nearly fifty other weeks of the year for business owners to find *thirsty* customers.

We've encouraged local businesses to focus on specific groups of *thirsty* people and promote a week or weekend in their honor. This can be done without putting on a festival or other large event as long as there are special offers and opportunities for these groups.

You'll see examples of on-going promotions by reading the weekly grocery store ads. One week the focus will be on baking items, the next week volunteerism, and after that seasonal suggestions or local events are highlighted. In each promotion, products are featured that coincide with the promotions. Many times, the promotions are built around a special manufacturer's purchase.

While promotions are certainly designed to benefit the customers, promotions also give business owners and relationship builders like you a reason to open your

mouth and tell everyone about your great promotions and products. You have to be your biggest promoter and then others will follow. Promote yourself and then others will, too.

✳ Publicity

Publicity is attracting attention about your business through various media without buying air time or advertising space; however, it takes concentrated time and persistent effort to get anything into the press. Publicity can be in the form of printed news releases for newspapers and magazines, which can also turn into featured stories. You can also gain publicity on radio, Internet, and television.

While your goal is to promote your product, editors and producers are looking for hooks to increase *thirsty* readers, viewers, and subscribers through unique stories and information.

Begin with small, local media by sending news releases, delivering samples, inviting reporters to a tour of your facility, or taking an editor or producer to lunch (each person has preferences on how to be contacted). I began my CookINspiration business by writing a cooking and inspirational column for my local paper and have developed a great relationship with the paper while generating a real following with the readers.

> Editors and producers are looking for hooks to increase *thirsty* readers, viewers, and subscribers through unique stories and information.

The key to publicity is to remember "It's not about me" (meaning you); it's about an awesome story!" Become a fan of the media you're pitching by doing a lot of leg work for them so their readership grows; then yours will, too.

✳ Purse/Pocket Presentations

In addition to or instead of carrying business cards, you can create a purse or pocket presentation you carry at all times. Use eight to ten 4" x 6" post cards with pictures of your products and announcements of new promotions along with three or four blank 4" x 6" index cards and a book ring to create this tool.

Use a hand-held hole punch to make holes in the upper corner of the cards, then thread the cards onto the book ring. You can put this on your key ring so you remember to always be watching for customers.

You now have a mini presentation to give *thirsty* people you meet. Once you do so, write the prospects' contact information on the blank index cards so you can follow through.

✳ Quick Questions

Asking quick questions for quick responses will capture a prospect's attention and you'll be able to know right away if someone is *thirsty* for what you are offering.

One question I *don't like* to use is, "Are you interested in..." The prospect doesn't really know if they have an interest because you haven't given them enough information, and so they usually say "no." The object here is to turn the major benefit of your product or service into a question that they respond to positively. Here are a few ideas:

Would you like to... (have more energy, cut your grocery bill in half, preserve your memories, have an extra hour a day)?

Have you received the free... (analysis, information, gift, catalog, product)? You know they haven't because you haven't sent it yet, but they are now thinking about your product or service.

Have you heard of... (the latest trend in fashion, book club, our specials this week/month)?

Do you want to learn how to... (speak a foreign language, cook gourmet meals in minutes, build a business in your spare time)?

✳ Quizzes

Put a humorous, short quiz on a website, handout, brochure or business card to entice more *thirsty* customers to contact you. When people can chuckle at the assessment of their "sour situation" they're ready to address it.

Here are sample questions which can be used for a variety of industries in which you're giving prospects a comparison of where they are to where they could be by using your products or services:

> When people can chuckle at the assessment of their "sour situation" they're ready to address it.

1. Do you have more boxes of product in your store than customers at your door?
2. Do you bounce checks more frequently than you balance your accounts?
3. Have you spent more time putting out fires than sparking your imagination?
4. Are you mistaken for your daughter or your mother?

Another quiz method is to ask yes and no questions and then proclaim, "If you answered yes to more than three of these statements, hurry and visit this website or call this phone number." In other words, encourage action.

✱ Raffles

My community held a fund raiser for a young man who is undergoing some extreme medical challenges. I had some products from one of my contractual clients that I was sure people would be *thirsty* to receive in the raffles.

Because of my tight schedule, I did not have enough time to set up a table as I normally would. In fact, I only had time to take the product I was donating along with a handful of catalogs and no door prize slips. The "sour situation" of not having enough preparation time became "juicy profits" for my direct sales client.

> Raffles can
> reap results!

Rather than creating a large display like other vendors, I simply put the set I was donating on the table where bags were lined up for people to deposit their raffle tickets according to which donated gift they hoped to win. And then I stayed next to my gift. This was a critical move. About 50 local merchants had donated gift certificates, products, and presents; most of these items were listed on a poster above the bags for the raffle tickets. Just a few items were actually displayed; these were the ones that had the most interest. However, I was the only representative who was in person to represent and demonstrate what I was donating.

As people walked by deciding which bag they wanted to put their raffle tickets in, I asked: "Do you love _____?" I did not say the name of the company; they would not have recognized it, or if they recognized the company name, they

might not have thought they were *thirsty* for what I was giving away. Instead, I asked if they loved the **category** of products.

For example: "Do you love scrapbooks?" (or clothes, makeup, decorating, cooking, stamping, candles, jewelry—whatever your product category.) If they said "no" I told them not to use their raffle ticket for my product because they wouldn't enjoy it. Some were stunned that I didn't try to *twist* their arm to listen to me; in fact, that actually created some intrigue.

If they said "yes" I took a couple of minutes to briefly explain how this product worked, which created a lot of interest. I found there were a lot of very *thirsty* people for what I was giving away. Several asked for a catalog. Remember, I only took a few of them—and I didn't take any door prize drawing forms at all. I was happy to give catalogs to people who would give me their names and phone numbers so I could contact them. I wrote this and any other pertinent information about them (one had just moved from California, another worked for the postal service, and so on) on my blank business cards.

Because this product was from a direct sales party plan client, once I knew these folks were *thirsty* for it, I asked, "Are you a Party Person?" This is more powerful than "Do you want to book a party?" Just like guests at a party, some were eager to say "yes" while some stated "no." However, I had eight people who asked me to call them about having a party. The next day, one of the ladies called my office and wanted to become a sales consultant.

My client was thrilled about the exposure we were able to give the company. So were the people I visited with, especially the person who opened a new business because we were happy to donate a product. Over the two years since then, more than 5,000 from that state joined that company as new sales consultants and thousands more had the opportunity to purchase the product because of one donated raffle gift.

✳ Real Estate Agents

Due to the many times that our family has relocated, we have met numerous real estate agents. I've discovered three common denominators among these professionals that can benefit relationship-based business owners and salespersons:

1. They know who is moving in from out of town. One way to get the names of new people in your city is from these agents. Create an alliance with a trusted, reliable agent to trade referrals. Just as they know the new people moving in, you might have friends and customers who are *thirsty* to list a home and can pass the referrals on to the agent you've aligned yourself with. Establish relationships with agents in a several different areas.

2. They're in more homes than most other professionals. When we recently listed our home, our agent was a terrific resource for professionals who repair fences, sell appliances, lay carpet, do inspections, and stage homes, among other things. If your business has any connection to what home sellers or buyers need, build a relationship with a real estate agent.

> Real estate professionals can be a great community and business resource.

3. They purchase housewarming gifts for their new buyers. In talking with agents as well as receiving gifts myself, $50-$75 is the average price that real estate agents pay for a housewarming gift. You deserve to have a piece of that pie! Before approaching an agent, prepare two or three different ideas or sets of products that you could offer. Giving a value-added price would be an incentive if the agent buys a certain quantity. The biggest advantage is the personal service you can give the busy agent. The added benefit is that you'll know another new customer—the new home buyer.

Here's a tip for all my Lemon Aid Learners who are real estate agents: Give your listing clients a listing gift. Yes, I can hear your objection right now: you haven't made any money off the deal yet, the contract could end before the house sells, and so on. However, if you give a gift up front that doubles as a selling tool, you're ahead of the game because the client's loyalty to you increases and the house might show better with the decoration, service, or scent you gave them.

If you don't personally know any real estate agents, getting their names is simple. Just pick up the free real estate magazines at the grocery stores. You'll find hundreds of names of agents! Even if they're not interested in creating this alliance or buying gifts, ask them if they would like your product for their personal use.

✱ Recipes

My favorite cookbooks in my vast library are those from ordinary home cooks who have used the recipes for years, using ingredients and techniques I'm familiar with. Each community, church, or club that has printed these volumes lists the contributor's name. If you belong to the organization that compiled a cookbook, look up the contributor's contact information in the organization's directory or website.

> Contact and congratulate contributors; every great cook loves a compliment!

Other cookbooks include recipes from home cooks across the nation, and their city and state are usually listed as well. If I like a recipe and feel like the contributor would be *thirsty* for my product, I look on line (world's biggest phone book). If I'm able to locate her information, I send her a fun thank you note along with my comments and a gift certificate, catalog or other marketing information.

Cookbooks created from recipe contests list similar information in addition to the award or recognition they won. If your product is related to kitchen tools and tasks, contact this potentially *thirsty* group and send a note of congrats; these winners deserve it!

✱ Records

When I visited the county seat to register my company name as a DBA (Doing Business As), I had to do my own search to be sure my chosen name was not already being used. As I did, I saw gallons and gallons of names listed on these records. Soon, I mentally did the *TWIST* and realized these are all business owners who need customers! They are certainly *thirsty* for my books and services! Could this be a *thirsty* group for your product?

Other public records could include building permits, business licenses, marriage licenses, divorce records, and real estate transactions. Determine if these records could contain names of *thirsty* people for your business. Each entity has different laws and rules governing access to these records.

❋ Referrals

A great benefit of having your own relationship-based business is that your customers tell others about you and your service, and your business grows exponentially! You've probably noticed by now that I haven't advised you to spend money on massive advertising campaigns. The ideas I've shared here cost very little in terms of dollars. The price you pay is giving outstanding service and follow through. You are your own best advertisement, and your customers are the next best billboard for your business.

Once you have completed the first business transaction with a customer, ask them who they know who would benefit from what you offer. I've found that by asking as soon as the transaction is made, I get more referrals; this is when the customer is at the height of excitement. Develop a system for immediately gathering and tracking the referrals. Writing directly on a sales receipt, order form, or contract has worked for me. When I return to my office, I put the name in my referral system file. Many times I've had customers ask me to wait to call their friends until they've had a chance to tell them about me. This suits me fine; all I ask is they let me know they've talked to their friends so I can follow through in a timely manner.

> Referrals are "free refills" for your business!

Give a referral gift to the referrer. If you choose to give a referral gift, it need not be expensive, but valuable to your client. A most meaningful token of appreciation is a sincere note of thanks and constant, exceptional service and follow through. The greatest intangible gift is giving great service to your customer's friends so your customer is esteemed, honored, and appreciated for introducing you to them.

❋ Restaurants

Do you offer a service or market a product a restaurant needs such as furniture, food preparation tools, stationery, food, pest control, cleaning services, etc.? Contact the owner and offer your personal service. If the restaurant is not a *thirsty* audience for your product, get permission to hang a flyer, leave literature, or have a business card bowl (use something more creative than a fish bowl) drawing for customers.

> **Hungry diners could be *thirsty* prospects.**

If you have to wait for a table, listen to the conversations of other people who are also in line. You'll be amazed at the contacts and connections you can make in this casual setting.

Get to know your server, too. Their experience ranges from part-time high school students to career-level professionals. The best are friendly and work to get to know what you're *thirsty* and hungry for. During your conversations, you can get to know more about them and the possibility of sharing your product or service to improve their lives. Many are also great sources for referrals if you frequent the restaurant and the wait staff knows you well.

❋ Rest Rooms

Anywhere you can have a captive audience, go for it! Hang flyers inside the rest room stall doors.

You might talk yourself out of this idea by rationalizing that the cleaning people will remove them. I've been in hundreds of restrooms and the one place that gets the least amount of attention is the inside of the door, as the maintenance staff would have to close themselves in the stall to do the job. I've watched many cleaners and have never seen this attention to detail. Even if the flyers are removed, you'll have an audience for a little while.

> **Rest Rooms are full of captive audiences.**

If your product is hand soap or lotion, leave bottles for the public to use along with business cards sitting next to the bottles.

❋ Retirement Homes

Retirement homes, not to be confused with nursing homes, are usually for healthy, older folks who don't want the hassle of owning their own home any longer, but want to be near their friends. As people grow older, many times they are less mobile.

Offer personalized service right at their retirement home. You can set up a

product display in an individual's apartment or in their social area. The people love this because they can shop and socialize without leaving their comfortable environment.

Retirement facilities I've worked with are always looking for ways to entertain the residents. If you can provide this with your product or sponsor a program, you'll have these people loving you!

✳ Reverse Selling

One of my more favorite ways of meeting new people is through reverse selling. This is when someone tells you about their product/service, and then you tell them about yours. Most sales people think of asking only their vendors to do business with them; instead, do a *TWIST*: anytime you are approached by another salesperson, listen to their information and decide to purchase or not. Then share your product information with them and if they are not *thirsty*, ask for referrals.

> You might not be *thirsty* for their product, but they could be *thirsty* for yours!

While I was doing my dishes one evening, I received a phone call from a telemarketer. She explained the purpose of her call and I listened carefully. I wasn't *thirsty* for whatever she offered me, and after stating such, I asked her if she enjoyed her telemarketing job. She said it was okay, but the pay wasn't all that great. I asked if she received commission on the sales she made and she replied that her pay was an hourly wage. I asked if she had to drive to work or made calls from home. She chuckled and said she wished she didn't have to drive to work. I told her that I worked from home calling prospects and selling products and earned hundreds of dollars a week. She was *thirsty!* She gave me her contact information (not all are allowed to do this) and joined my company.

If you can't get the name and home phone numbers at that time, give her your website address, phone number or e-mail. Some people will contact you, depending on how *thirsty* they are!

Think reverse selling when you read advertisements, listen to TV and radio ads,

read direct mail pieces, flyers, bulletin boards, and want ads. Keep asking yourself, "How can I give aid to this person with my product?" You'll find people and businesses to service that you would not have found otherwise.

You can use reverse selling when people ask you about purchasing something for their fund raiser. Listen to them and what they have to offer, then tell them about your fund raising program.

✳ "Same Name"

When I meet someone with my same name— either first or last—I feel a real affinity for that person. And, if they spell their name the same way I do, it's stronger (like the way Christie Brinkley spells hers!). The better I get to know that person the more I can teach them how to solve their problems. Anytime you have a commonality with someone, they tend to listen to you more and are more open to your ideas.

✳ Samples and Sips

If you're not sure if you want regular lemonade or strawberry lemonade, you might want a "sip" of each before deciding. I love sharing "sips" of my concepts in my newsletters; subscribers get a feel for what I teach.

If you have small packages of your product to give away, do so. If you don't have samples, consider breaking apart some product sets so you can give "sips" to prospects. So, when you meet someone, you can ask, "Did you get the free sample of my XYZ product?" This great question creates a conversation because most people are *thirsty* to try something for free. As you hand the samples to the prospect, assure them that you'll follow up so they can buy the full size right away. Then they're eager to share their contact information, and you're on your way to sampling a new customer.

> Sample a new customer by giving away samples.

171

✳ Schools

If you're a teacher, administrator or a volunteer at a school, you could have a never-ending source of new leads.

Teachers: They're real people and they shop just like everyone else. What's unique about your product that would entice a teacher to want it? Is your product related to a subject that they teach? What about a business opportunity or sales position in your company? Because selling is really teaching, teachers can excel in this role, particularly in seasonal positions as well as those with flexible hours, as most teachers work at school only nine of the twelve months.

> Selling is simply teaching.

Volunteers: Sometimes people volunteer because they're looking for something else to do—and that's not a bad position to be in! However, volunteers do not get paid; your opportunity might be something they can do along with the volunteer work and give them a paycheck.

Volunteer yourself: When I've been a room mother, I met other moms, told them about my business, and started new customer bases. When appropriate, I handed small samples of my product out with the holiday treats. You can also volunteer to teach a class on a subject related to your business. For example, if you sell books, offer to do a special story hour. Maybe you could bring your book display in and let the children leaf through them for an hour or so.

Fund Raisers: Schools are always looking for ways to raise more money. I've found that going to individual class rooms and departments (music, athletics, and so forth) in the school is much easier to secure a fund raiser event than going through committees and boards.

School Directories: Use your child's school directory to contact parents about your business and product. You can mail or e-mail information, or make calls (personal contact always has more impact.)

✳ Service

This book contains literally hundreds of ideas of finding new leads so your business—and your checkbook—can grow. This is the simplest, yet most important, concept of the entire book. Giving excellent service to your customers is the most important way to grow your business. When you do so for just one customer, she will brag about you to her friends and acquaintances, and you'll forever be in business!

> Giving excellent service to your customers is the most important way to grow your business.

Customer service is talked about today more than ever, but it's seldom really practiced! Even if you have only a few customers right now, keep your promises, deliver more than they expect, and do your very best to solve their problems with your products or service and they will remember and refer you.

✳ Service Providers

Every service person who comes to my home to repair my washer, install new blinds, mow my lawn, or perform any other service is introduced to my business. When someone is on my turf, I get to know more about them than if I were visiting elsewhere.

Your service people will see your company's products if they are used or displayed in your home, office, or yard; they'll often ask you about them before you have an opportunity to share your goods or services with them.

Service providers are also in many homes and businesses as a course of their work, so they can be a wonderful referral source when they see you might have the sweet solution to another client's sour situation. Additionally, when the service person performs to your standards, you can be a referral source for him or her as well.

✳ Shopping Bags

Shopping has now become a sport to many people, and these "shopaholics" love to collect creative shopping bags. I confess I've made purchases at stores just to get their fun bag!

While your colorful, creative shopping bag might be a collectible for your customers, you'll also be able to collect more customers because your bags become *wonderful billboards for your business*. When other shoppers see your customers carrying your bag, they are introduced to your company.

Produce bags with your company's logo and slogan. Or, purchase solid-colored plastic bags representing your company. For example, when you attend one of my live Lemon Aid Learning Adventures, you'll take your Lemon Aid home in a bright yellow plastic bag. Every time you use and reuse the bag (another benefit of shopping bags), you'll remember your Lemon Aid experience.

If you don't have your own branded shopping bag, purchase clear plastic bags so your product will be visible to the world.

✳ Sponsorship Opportunities

> You don't need to have a huge company or live in a large city to be a sponsor.

The more often your company's name is in front of the public, the more exposure you'll have and thus, the more customers you'll gain. You can get this recognition when your company sponsors a person, event, chair, room, scholarship, and as we've all seen on college and medical campuses, buildings!

You don't need to have a huge company or live in a large city to be a sponsor. In the small towns I've lived in, sponsorships abound. One such event is a fancy gala to raise scholarship funds. There are varying levels of sponsorships, some as little as twenty dollars. Your company is recognized as a sponsor and you're benefitting a good cause.

The *TWIST* to this is you can seek sponsors yourself for a product, an event you're holding, an advertisement you're placing, or a race car you're driving. Once again, the list is limited only by your willingness to ask a person or business to sponsor you.

When you do have a sponsor, always give appreciation and represent your sponsor well.

✳ Sports Teams

Are you a soccer mom or dad? What about baseball, basketball, bowling and so on? As you watch your children participate in sports, you normally meet and talk with other parents.

On the other hand, you might be a volunteer coach or umpire. So, let coaches and parents know about your business! Use your product so they can see it whenever possible or practical. Your company could sponsor a team event or uniform.

> Finding customers is a great contact sport!

If you, your spouse, or both of you are the athlete(s), you're already close to other team members. Most teams have a few social events during the season. Tell these folks about what you do; always ask for referrals as well. These groups will open up hundreds of lead avenues for you! Of course, be willing to tell your associates about the businesses your team members may have; this way, you are really networking.

✳ Telephone

Look at your telephones as your cash registers. Every time you dial a prospect's number, or someone calls you, listen to the cha-ching, cha-ching of the money going through.

> Your *thirsty* customers are carrying their phones with them!

With the huge increase of e-mail and texting, you might think the telephone is no longer a tool for finding customers; especially if you have a bad case of *Phone Phobia*—fear of the telephone. Quite the opposite is true as the number of telephones, specifically cell phones, has multiplied over the last decade. The great news is your *thirsty* customers are carrying their phones with them—no longer do you have to catch them at home or wonder when they'll be available. Pick up the phone and dial!

Outbound calls: While you might play phone tag, your name and phone number will show up on caller ID, so your prospects will know you're attempting to contact them.

One way you can demonstrate a courtesy is by beginning every conversation with an important question, and I don't mean the overused "How are you?" The question is:

"Am I getting you at a good time?"

176

This question conveys that you respect the prospect's time and are gaining permission to continue the conversation. It's also more positive and confident than asking, "Is this a bad time to talk to you?"

Another opening question to avoid is: "Are you busy?" Most people are busy and don't have time to listen to a question like this. Plus, it's easy for people to say "Yes", which signals the call is not welcome; you then politely say goodbye.

If you want to be more specific you might do a *TWIST* and ask:

"Is this a good time to talk for just _____ minutes?"

Fill in the blank with the number of minutes you think the conversation will take; I recommend a prospecting call be no longer than five minutes. This approach works well when you call someone who never seems to have time to talk; you're giving an implied promise to take only the amount of time you proposed. You can also use this idea when you call someone who likes to talk a lot; you've just announced that your time is limited.

> Prospects and customers don't always call you even if they are very *thirsty* for your product.

In either case, you keep your promise to engage the person in conversation only for that designated amount of time. If you see the limit is approaching, say, "I promised I'd keep you for only five minutes. Can we schedule another appointment to finish discussing the details of this proposal?"

News Flash: Prospects and customers don't always call you even if they are very *thirsty* for your product. They want to, but like you, have other things on their calendar. That's why you must create a system where you can make regular phone calls to thank customers for their orders, check to be sure they love your product, and to ask for referrals and future business. Yes, you can do some of this communicating with e-mail, texting, or letters and notes; however, one of the best ways to connect with prospects and customers is a two-way, real-time conversation. If, however, a prospect has asked you to connect in a specific way—say by e-mail—honor that request.

As you consistently work to find and keep customers by using the telephone, you'll soon see that the inbound calls begin to increase: more people call you to

purchase your product, and these calls are not from the people you called and left messages with. Yes, it does seem unrealistic. But it happens! Try this experiment; you'll see that it really does work this way.

When you dial a number and get a voice mail greeting, do not hang up; always leave a message. After all, the recipient of your call probably has caller ID and will wonder why you didn't leave a message; she might even call you up to see what you wanted. Refer to the letter V in this alphabet to learn the best ways to leave voice mail messages.

> More phone calls equal more customers!

Inbound calls: Whenever your business phone rings, answer it as if you just won the lottery (excitement) and identify yourself and your company clearly. These phone calls are essentially auditions; if the caller is impressed with you or your employees, they'll be ready to do business with you. If you act as if the call is an interruption, the caller will feel that as well.

The more calls you have coming in, the more money you'll make; this is why your telephone is a virtual cash register. I suggest getting connected to a voice mail system so your prospects can leave a message if you're not available. For businesses, I don't recommend using call-interrupting (also known as call waiting). I have my voice mail set up so that if I'm on the phone and another call comes in, the new call goes directly to voice mail. This way, the customer I'm talking with doesn't get interrupted, and I can call the other person back right away.

✳ Testimonials

A couple of weeks ago, my book club sent me an e-mail about a three-day special. I wasn't in the market for another book, but decided to shop anyway; sure enough, I found a book that sounded intriguing. The "deal maker" which prompted me to click on the "order" button was reading the testimonials of those who had purchased the book. As I read the positive, specific comments, I knew I'd like the book, and I did. In fact, I've already recommended it to a handful of my friends.

When my wonderful Lemon Aid Learners send me unsolicited e-mails or call to share the results they've achieved from listening to and implementing my ideas,

I thank them for their comments and then ask if I can have permission to use their feedback in my marketing materials. Additionally, when I visit with customers, many say they order based on the testimonials they've read on my literature or websites.

When I began my presentation and consulting business, I used to solicit comments and received a lot of compliments. However, I soon found that the most valuable words for prospects are reading the experiences from people creating specific results, not just their opinions from sitting at a class or reading a book.

> Testimonials can be the deal maker.

What are your customers raving about after using your product? Have they eliminated sour situations in their lives and want to tell the world about you? Don't be shy; ask them! And let their testimonials benefit your prospects.

✲ Texting

If you know your prospects use text messaging, use it. Texting is a great way to communicate quick bits of information to them, such as the launch of a new product, an invitation to an exclusive event, the announcement of a spectacular sale, or notification that their order has been shipped or delayed.

How do you know if texting is appropriate? Ask them! This can be done when customers order or fill out a door prize slip at an event. Some of my friends are not happy to receive marketing texts since they pay per text message received, so get permission to use this type of communication.

> A sure way to know if someone is a "texter" is if he sends the first text.

A sure way to know if someone is a "texter" is if he sends the first text. When you receive this, you know he approves of texting and possibly prefers that form of communication.

Texting has its own shorthand and codes, which might be okay for personal use. However, for business purposes, it's best to spell out words so that your message is clear.

You can also do a *TWIST* for "text-a-holic" customers and create a marketing message with text language unique to your product or offer.

✻ Thank You Notes

One of the most powerful ways to find and keep *thirsty* customers is to send notes of appreciation. When someone has been helpful to me when I'm the customer, I love to send them a "thanks for great service" note. When I do, I always enclose my business card so they remember who I am. Often, they'll call to find out more about what I do. After all, if they are a service person to me, they'll want my business to grow to keep them in business.

> Thank you notes cement relationships and encourage referrals.

You'll certainly want to send notes to customers who have placed orders as well as to prospects who have visited your booth or listened to a sales presentation. Thank you notes cement relationships and encourage referrals.

✻ Tours

Humans are curious beings, and they especially love to know what goes on behind the scenes; that's why movie studios make big bucks charging people to tour their facilities.

To entice prospects to find out more about your company, open your business once or twice a year for tours. This is a great idea when you host a Grand Opening of your company, and also works well if your business is something kids would enjoy attending on a school field trip.

Tours don't have to be lengthy or extravagant. Prospects might be *thirsty* to see how orders are received from your website and how product is shipped. Obviously, if you have trade secrets or potentially dangerous equipment, don't take people to those areas.

Give each person an advertising souvenir to remind them of the tour and of your business.

* Uniqueness

Buy a bag of lemons and examine each one. They appear to be the same with their uniform size and constant color. However, you will see that each is unique; especially when you cut the fruit open and see each lemon has a different thickness of peel and a unique number of seeds inside.

Customers are like lemons; they might look similar but each one is unique. One of the greatest benefits of relationship-based businesses is that you get to know your customers on a very personal level so you can customize your products, services, and ideas to their needs and wants. You can find out what they are really *thirsty* for. In fact, you might develop a product or program based on one individual's requests that other customers will also love.

> Know and celebrate your unique customers and they'll remember you.

When you look for the unique traits and characteristics of your customers, you'll remember who they really are, and that makes *you* a unique vendor, supplier, or business professional in your customers' eyes. And that uniqueness you possess is what will cause them to remember you when they or someone they know wants your product. Uniqueness strengthens your business and personal relationships, and attracts more *thirsty* people to do business with you.

✳ Universities

You'll be amazed at the kinds of contacts you'll find on a college campus. Having recently returned to college to work on a second degree, I've found this to be a potential gold mine. Here's why you should consider "attending" (or at least visiting) a university to find prospects:

1. Advertising is cheap if you want to pay for a classified or display ad in the student paper.

2. Upon approval by the school, you can hang flyers.

3. College students can be eager recruits or employees. They are young (or young at heart), enthusiastic, and need money along with a very flexible schedule.

4. College students are very innovative. The ideas for posting flyers in bathroom stalls come from my recent college experience.

5. Local students will refer you to other people in the area, many times their parents, for future business.

6. Campus clubs are filled with specific groups of students who might be your *thirsty* audience.

7. Many colleges have career/job fairs. You can put a display here for a very minimal charge, if any.

8. Registering for classes that could be related—even distantly—to your business allows you to meet other professionals, learn from them, and invite them to do business with you. And don't rule out the instructors. They could become prospects too, so let them know about your business.

✳ Value

A good friend owns several rental properties and was concerned when one was vacant during a downturn in his local market. He asked me if he should lower the price to compete with other rentals. My suggestion was to add value to the home so he would still get the rent while the renters got more in return compared to other places.

He put in some new appliances and painted the home. Because he added value to the property, he quickly found a tenant who was happy to pay the asking price because they saw the greater value.

We've bought and sold several homes and in some cases our agent suggested we lower the price if we didn't have an offer within a few weeks. However, my "fill-osophy" is to add value rather than to reduce prices. Yes, we all love a great deal, but when we make bargains out of our offer, the value is reduced.

> Bargains are not always valuable.

You'll attract more *thirsty* customers when you show the value of working with you and purchasing your product rather than reducing the price; that just reduces its perceived value. This is not to say you should not offer incentives and specials; customers love great values. You'll know you're reducing value to create a bargain when you convey a desperate outlook and begin begging for business. Your prospects will feel it as they prefer to work with persons and companies of value.

❋ Vendors

Which companies or individuals do you do business with for both your business as well as your personal needs? My slogan is "I do business with people who do business with me." Are the following people part of your customer base: insurance representative, mechanic, child care provider, attorney, dry cleaner, hair stylist... The list is almost endless.

Go through your checkbook—both business and personal—to see who you've written checks to. Have these people or businesses written one to you for your services? If they aren't part of your customer base, have you told them about your business?

> Are your vendors your customers?

At one point, I was taking my sons to the doctor's office very regularly. When I got to the billing desk to pay, I gave the office workers (who always said they were *thirsty* for my products but never ordered) a catalog and asked which of my products they wanted. The woman who was helping me looked surprised. I said, "Hey, I've been writing checks to you regularly, now you can write one to me." They all laughed, agreed, and placed an order!

Remember that some of your vendors might already have someone servicing them with your type of product or service. Don't harass them; just keep in touch to be sure they are happy with their present vendor, and if not, let them know what you can do for them.

❋ Veterinary

People with "four-legged children" love their animals! Companies are now providing health insurance to dogs and cats. This is such a huge market that new direct sales companies have even been formed over the past five years to satisfy a very *thirsty* market: pet owners.

Do you have a product that is complimentary to a veterinarian? You might make hair accessories to market to salons. Can you do the *TWIST* and create them for

pets? Are you an accomplished knitter? Why not knit items for animals? Begin by doing some cross-promoting with the animal doctor.

✳ Videos

If you want *thirsty* people to get to know you and your products and services, post a video on your website, Facebook page, blog, or video site such as YouTube. The videos need to be short and contain ideas and tips (I call mine "sips") so you'll create a *thirst* for what you offer. Be sure to include a graphic of your website, phone number, or e-mail on the video so prospects can contact you immediately.

> Videos are a great way to "show and sell."

✳ Voice Mail

You can attract *thirsty* customers by the way you leave messages and create voice mail greetings.

Leaving a message on outbound calls: The rule is to always leave a message. Years ago, I would hang up on answering machines because I was afraid the people wouldn't be happy that I called—I had to change my paradigm and up my belief in myself and my product! Believe in what you're doing, and others will be thrilled to hear from you.

The next reason I leave a message is because so many people have caller identification; they'll know you called even if you didn't want them to know! Leave a message that will make them want to return your call. I have left messages that say:

"I have to tell you some news you've been waiting for."

"I have a surprise for you." (People love surprises and want to know what the surprise is—now!)

"You won't believe what I have to tell you!"

Because my prospects and customers are busy people, I don't expect them to call me, so I state:

> "I'll be calling you back, or if you just can't wait for that, you can call me first. My phone number is 555-553-1212."

And, do call them back, if you can beat them to the phone. Very often, people will call you because they want to know your news!

Leaving messages works well on cold calls because if the people are *thirsty* for your offer, they really will call you back. If not, you've wasted little time and energy. In this case, my script is a little bit different:

> "This is Christie calling from _____(your company). We have a half-price offer this month. To find out more, call me at _____(your number)."

> Create a voice mail greeting with an awesome advertisement!

Voice Mail Greeting for incoming calls: Leave an advertisement on your voice mail so that when people call you, they'll hear about your business and current promotions. You're paying for your phone regardless if you do an advertisement or not, so you might as well benefit from incoming calls.

I call a lot of people who have home-based businesses and am surprised that only a small number of these have advertisements on their voice mail greeting. Hurry now and create an advertisement that will cause great interest in your product and opportunity. Change the message often, and don't keep a message with old news.

✳ Waiting Areas

If you find yourself in a waiting room, that means that you're doing business with some kind of a professional, be this a hair stylist, attorney, dentist, chiropractor or many other professional services. Because you have to wait for your appointment just as the other customers, take time to get to know them. Start a conversation by asking leading questions; listen to what they tell you all about themselves. Determine if you can solve their "sour situations" with your product/service.

Catalogs are great entertainment for people in waiting areas.

If your product is something that people can use while waiting for their appointment—such as games, magazines, books, or toys—donate these to the owner for use in the waiting room in exchange for permission to leave business cards, a display, flyers or catalogs in the waiting room.

Carry a basket with some of your products; this will arouse some curiosity. If you can use your product while you're waiting, other people may ask where you found it.

You're patronizing a business so give them the opportunity to do business with you! If you have a product catalog, leave a couple on the tables.

✳ Website Tour

In the segment on *Internet*, I talked about having websites. Here I'll discuss taking your prospects on a website tour.

If you wanted to show off your company or office to customers by taking them on a tour, wouldn't you want to be their tour guide so they'd know where to go? We're in the process of choosing a new health insurance policy. One of my concerns is if the network has a large choice of providers. When I asked the agent this question, she, like so many other salespersons said, "Check out the website." When I went to the site, I could not find where a non-customer could gain access to this information; there were tabs and links all over the place, it was very confusing. I ended up wasting my time and left her "store."

> Always be on the same page— literally!

A website also represents your company, but when you give out your web address, most people will not take time to visit. However, if you follow up and invite them to take a tour *with* you, the response and results will be much greater.

You can take customers on a tour while you're talking on the phone, visiting with them in person, or while chatting on line. Obviously, you'll begin at the home page. Be sure they are on the right page to start; one incorrect letter will take them to a different site or give them an error message.

As you move them from page to page, always be sure you're both on the *same page*. I look for something that's easily identifiable and say, "Are you on the page with the green rectangle in the center with the purple text that reads "Sale?" It's easy to get tangled in a website!

Find out what your customer is *thirsty* for. Does she want to view your weekly specials, look over your menu, or create her own set of your products? While websites have site maps, each also has anomalies that to you as the owner seem obvious, yet to a prospect or customer could be confusing. And when someone is confused, they'll click and leave.

Once you know which area your prospect wants to visit, show some pages of your site they might never have found on their own.

If you have a newsletter, be sure the prospect subscribes if they haven't already. Have them list your site in their "Favorites" folder or bookmark your site.

If you haven't met them before, take the prospect to the pages that tell about you or your company's background. I love to visit a person's site and see their picture while I'm talking on the phone with them. When your prospect sees photos of you or your facilities, she has a greater connection with you.

Do you have a membership site? Demonstrate how that works. Do you have free materials prospects can download? Where can they find that? If they need to know your hours or schedule, show them where they'll find that information. Do you have archives of articles or videos they'd love to read and watch?

If you provide a service that requires the customer to download forms or open files for electronic signatures before a policy can be opened or contract secured, offer to take the prospect through each step to the point where everything is filled out and the forms are e-mailed to you. Wait patiently while they go through this process, otherwise they might abandon the deal.

Of course, the best part of a website is the shopping center! Find out which items your prospect is *thirsty* for. Click on the category and offer some suggestions. Before you complete your tour, demonstrate how the checkout process works, which credit cards you accept and your turn-around time to ship an order, and if and how the order can be tracked. At this point you could give the prospect an exclusive gift code which is valid only that day.

> Offer to walk your customer through on line processes so they successfully complete the transaction.

Not every customer will want a tour, but be prepared to give one so they'll want to return to your website and shop more and more. And as you tour your site with your prospect, you'll see things from a customer's point of view that you might want to change so it's more user-friendly.

✳ Wedding Lists

Wedding lists are full of family and friends, some you only see at once-in-a life-time events but want to share special days with. Perhaps, like me, you've been married over thirty years to the same person. If you were to have a wedding cele-bration, who would you invite? Would these people want to celebrate your busi-ness with you as well? Would they be *thirsty* for your product?

As my three sons have married, and we've planned their wedding receptions, I enjoyed going through the lists of our family and friends to invite as many of them as possible to the celebration.

Use these lists to remind you of your relationships with people you might not see all the time, yet who could be *thirsty* to know more about your business, and would love to celebrate your successes with you.

✳ Welcome Baskets

> Welcome new customers with baskets of samples and information.

Welcome new members of your neighborhood, church, school, community, or club by delivering a basket of your product samples and literature. Include pertinent informa-tion about your community as well, especially a map where you'll highlight your place of business.

Consult with your local Chamber of Commerce to see what materials they will give you to add to the welcome baskets; talk to other business owners. Check with real estate agents to know which homes have been sold recently so you can deliver baskets to people outside of the groups listed above.

✳ Winners

After complimenting my neighbor on her new window treatments, she excitedly told me she'd won a great deal at a recent home expo she had attended. She further explained that she entered a drawing and even though she wasn't the

grand prize winner, she was offered a "runner up" great value on window treatments. You can call some of your customers every day and let them know they've "won" a great value that you offer only to these folks.

You've read other segments in this book about choosing winners in business card drawings, electronic newsletter winners, or at vendor events; after you've notified the winners, post their names on your website. Ask their permission to do so, and they'll have extra recognition as being one of your winners!

Post the names of winners on your website along with a photo of them with their gift.

✳ Word of Mouth

Relationship-based businesses are all about word-of-mouth advertising. Most business owners, salespeople and independent consultants like you have limited (if any) advertising budgets. You don't need it! Instead, your customers will open their mouths and tell their family and friends about your awesome products and terrific service. Be good to your customers and they'll tell the world about you.

✳ Xceptional Xamples

You must become a "product" of your product if you expect others to buy what you sell. Be the best example of your product or service that anyone has ever seen. If you sell Mercedes-Benz cars, for example, be sure you own one yourself! Nothing speaks like the voice of experience. People will believe you more and do business with you more often with you when you *walk your talk*!

✳ Yard Signs

For home-based companies, put a sign on your front yard with your company name and logo so passers-by will know where they can get your product or service. Your website should be listed as well.

The side benefit is that when the neighbors give directions to their friends about how to get to their house, they'll use your sign as a reference. "Turn right at the house with the XYZ sign." You'll be happily amazed at the new people you'll meet.

✳ Year Books

Contact your local schools and dance clubs about their end-of-year year books: You can advertise in them! The best way is if one of your children happens to attend the school. You can place a good wish message to students while advertising your business. If you don't have children in these groups, ask about advertising anyway, and stipulate that you want a list of people who are members of the group so you can follow up.

✳ Yellow Pages

At one point in my sales career, I was ready for a big *TWIST!* So I responded to an ad for advertising sales at a radio station. I had no experience selling air time, but

was ready to take on a new challenge. The station was new and offered no training; I even wrote the commercials and recorded the spots.

Within a couple days, I had a new client: an art gallery. I was proud of my accomplishment in a new field and bragged to my brother about the victory. He caught on to my prospecting method quickly of using the yellow pages from A (art gallery) to Z to find *thirsty* prospects.

> Yellow pages can be a *golden* treasure of leads!

If your product or service is something other businesses could be *thirsty* for, check out the yellow pages of your local phone book where businesses are listed according to their category. If your *thirsty* audience is a tutoring service, look for them under "Tutoring." If you don't have a hard copy of a telephone book, do a Google search to find the yellow page directories in your area.

✳ Youth Groups

Marketing experts know that 'tweens and teens are one of the best demographics to market to. Likewise, many groups and organizations are formed around the needs and desires of kids in these age brackets. Check with your community, church, school or sports organizations to find parents, leaders, and youth who are *thirsty* for what you offer.

Perhaps your business is planning after school events or organizing accommodations for sports team travel. You could also market your services to bands or cheer squads. Kids are typically much more tech-savvy than parents, so be knowledgeable and prepared to "speak their language" so you don't come across as a boring adult.

✳ Zillions of other Ideas

As this "alphabet" ends, remember that this is just the beginning of a process of finding new lead ideas that you'll develop yourself as you try out the suggestions in this book. The world is full of links. By starting with these leads—which are the seeds—you'll be linked to an infinite amount of ideas and leads. You'll never be out of business—even if you do run out of family and friends.

> Use this Lemon Aid Lead Alphabet and you'll never be out of business—even if you do run out of family and friends.

TWISTs I've Created
to Find More Customers

Now that you've used the Lemon Aid tips, what new ideas have you come up with?

New Customers I've Found after Using this Book

Invite your new customers to autograph this page.

Thirsty for More Lemon Aid?

Check out these other books, presentations, and websites
by Christie Northrup, The Lemon Aid Lady™.

BOOKS

CookINspiration: Recipes with an inspirational message, taught in Pair-A-Bowls.
Great gift idea! Visit CookINspiration.com

Presentations for Profits: Home party plan consultants will learn how
to attract, not attack, more hosts at parties. Visit LemonAidLady.com

Team Themes 2: Captivate your sales team with fun, interactive
meetings, invitations, and awards. Visit LemonAidLady.com

Best of The Lemon Aid Lady: Seasonal suggestions and creative
"sips" from *The Lemon Aid Stand for Party Plan* newsletter.
Visit LemonAidLady.com

PRESENTATIONS AND WORKSHOPS

Where and How to Find More Customers when You Run Out of Family and Friends
Based on the contents of this book and customized to your company's *thirst*

CookINCommunication
Learn communication and connection recipes to create a professional, yet personable, image
while you attract and keep more customers and clients

Totally Terrific Teams
How to encourage, inspire, educate, and influence positive and professional team members

Lemon Aid for Leaders
Learn Lemon Aid Leadership Laws and put them into practice so your business is like a lemon
tree, never a dormant season, always blossoming and producing!

Visit **WhereToFindCustomers.com** for more "sips" and *TWISTs*

To discuss your needs or to schedule Christie
for your next event, call Lemon Aid Learning Adventures
217-453-6007 or e-mail Ideas@LemonAidLady.com

Get More when you Order More

If you lead a sales team or do business in multiple locations, you need more copies of *Where–and How–to Find Customers.* Take advantage of The Lemon Aid Lady's special offers:

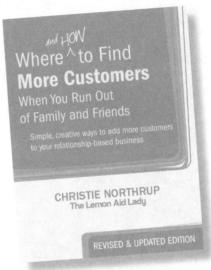

Order **50 or more** copies of this book and get FREE SHIPPING

Buy **500 or more copies** and Christie will visit your location for a complimentary two-hour presentation; just pay for her travel expenses.

Purchase **1,000 or more copies**, your company will receive a **FREE**, customized insert and cover–and Christie will still come to speak to your group.

Thirsty? Give the Lemon Aid Lady a call

at 217-453-6007

or e-mail Ideas@LemonAidLady.com

WhereToFindCustomers.com

Offer subject to change.